D1824500

# 100 Ideas for Primary Teachers:

# Daily Reflections

# Other titles in the 100 Ideas for Primary Teachers series

# 100 Ideas for Primary Teachers:

# Daily Reflections

## Adam Bushnell

BLOOMSBURY EDUCATION

LONDON OXFORD NEW YORK NEW DELHI SYDNEY

BLOOMSBURY EDUCATION

Bloomsbury Publishing Plc

50 Bedford Square, London, WC1B 3DP, UK

29 Earlsfort Terrace, Dublin 2, Ireland

BLOOMSBURY, BLOOMSBURY EDUCATION and the Diana logo are trademarks of Bloomsbury Publishing Plc

First published in Great Britain 2024 by Bloomsbury Publishing Ltd
This edition published in Great Britain 2024 by Bloomsbury Publishing Ltd

A catalogue record for this book is available from the British Library

ISBN: PB: 978-1-8019-9292-3; ePDF: 978-1-8019-9291-6; ePub: 978-1-8019-9294-7

2 4 6 8 10 9 7 5 3 1 (paperback)

Typeset by Newgen KnowledgeWorks Pvt. Ltd., Chennai, India
Printed and bound in the UK by CPI Group (UK) Ltd, Croydon, CR0 4YY

MIX
Paper | Supporting
responsible forestry
FSC® C013604

To find out more about our authors and books visit www.bloomsbury.com and sign up for our newsletters.

# Contents

# Acknowledgements

Many thanks to my friends and family for your continued support. Thanks to Marie Parkinson and Debbie Hamilton for their involvement in the book. Thanks also to Ghazala Malik and all my friends at Westbourne Primary School. Many thanks as well to Dr Sandra Witton, Helen Rice and all my friends at Finchale Primary School. Thanks also to the amazing team at Bloomsbury for your hard work and patience.

# Introduction

The Oxford dictionary definition of the noun 'reflection' in the context of this book is 'serious thought or consideration about something'. The definition of the verb 'reflect' is 'to think deeply or carefully'.

In these daily reflections, we will be considering a subject and then giving children the time to reflect on it. We can reflect on them too, and consider how to incorporate the ideas into a daily classroom routine. The goal of this book is to help children develop their self-esteem, empathy, resilience and perseverance. Reflecting daily on important subjects such as kindness and self-awareness can help children to find clarity on these subjects. When children focus on kindness and self-awareness, they can build upon and develop their understanding of themselves and others. Life can be unpredictable and these reflections give children practical mental tools for dealing with life's uncertainties. A daily dose of guided philosophical reflection can help children to be optimistic and feel positive about their lives.

Each reflection is specifically designed to help children's mental health by giving daily advice on how to be positive, take on new challenges, feel confident, be relaxed, feel happy, be friendly, be supportive and work as a team. Forgiveness and gentleness, both to oneself and others, are recurring themes too. The reflections can be shared in assemblies, with the whole class, small groups or individuals. The quotation and opening sentence tell you what the reflection is about. Occasionally, you might find it useful to read the quote to the children as well. The reflection follows in italics. This text should be read aloud to the children. After the reflection text, you'll find a prompt or activity to use in the classroom, and there are then either teaching tips or suggestions as to how to take the reflection further. Once you've finished reading the reflection, before moving on to the next activity, either allow some quiet time for the children to individually consider what you have just read to them or give them some discussion time in pairs, groups or as a class.

I wrote this book as we seem to be at a mental health crisis point in the UK. So, what can we do as educators to help children with their wellbeing? It is my belief that we urgently need more emphasis put on mental wellbeing in primary education in order to give children the tools they need to battle anxiety in later life. By practising the recommendations in these reflections, children will be able to look at life more positively and with gratitude for what they have. The readings attempt to encourage us all to live in the here and now. If, however, you are concerned about a child's mental health then it is important to discuss this with your designated mental health lead.

The aim of these reflections is to empower you and the children you work with to live better lives, and to provide everyday tools to help you to become calmer and happier.

The reflections are split into four parts: self-awareness, doing good, choice and life lessons. The reason for this is to encourage children to reflect upon themselves first, then consider the freedom they have to do good things, followed by making positive choices in their lives and finally, what they can learn from every experience.

So, breathe deeply, relax, smile and be grateful as often as you can.

Enjoy!

# How to use this book

This book includes quick, easy and practical ideas for you to dip in and out of to help you promote children's mental health and wellbeing.

Each idea includes:

- a catchy title that is easy to refer to and share with your colleagues
- an interesting quote linked to the idea
- a summary of the idea in bold, making it easy to flick through the book and identify an idea you want to use at a glance
- a reflection to read aloud to the class in italics
- a prompt or activity to use next.

Each idea also includes one or more of the following:

### Teaching tip

Practical tips and advice for how and how not to run the activity or put the idea into practice.

### Taking it further

Ideas and advice for how to extend the idea or develop it further.

### Bonus idea ★

There are 12 bonus ideas in this book that are extra-exciting, extra-original and extra-interesting.

Share how you use these ideas and find out what other practitioners have done using **#100ideas**.

# Self-awareness

**Part 1**

# Things we can change

'What can I do to change the world?'

**Help children to focus on what things about themselves and the world they would like to change.**

**Taking it further**

Ask the children to think about what bigger things they would like to change about the world. You could make a list and choose some of their ideas to expand upon. If the children mention helping the environment, you could visit the Greenpeace website together and look for ideas about how you, as a school, could help the environment.

*Is there something in the world that you want to change? Is it to do with animals and the environment? Is it to do with homelessness or poverty? Or is it something to do with yourself? Perhaps you want to get better at football, gymnastics or reading.*

*Some things are impossible to change. You can't make yourself taller or shorter, or make your nose longer or shorter. However, you can get better at activities. The more you practise a certain activity, the better you get at it. Nobody is born good at playing football, performing gymnastic routines or being able to read a book. It takes time and effort to improve these skills, but the rewards of scoring a goal, completing a cartwheel or finishing a book are so worth it.*

*But can we really make changes to the world? We really can! There are lots of things you can do to help people, from donating to food banks to giving charity shops a bag of unwanted clothes or toys.*

*What do you want to change and how will you do it?*

Discuss with the children what small things they can do to change the world. You can make suggestions such as holding a door open, picking up litter or even just smiling more often.

# Things we cannot change

'Life is happening right now!'

**Give children the chance to reflect on the things they can't change and teach them the importance of acceptance.**

There are things that you can't change and that's just part of life. These things might annoy you, like getting too much homework, but every child in school gets homework. Homework is part of school life. You can't make school stop setting homework just like you can't make somebody like you and want to be your best friend. There are things in life that we just have to accept.

Accepting the things we cannot change helps to build self-confidence. Try out the following:

- Think about what makes you... you. What makes you special?
- Work out the things you are good at.
- Do things that make you feel happy.
- Set yourself challenges.
- Think positively.
- Let go of the things you cannot change.

If you try your best to practise those six things regularly, you can build your self-confidence over time. The last one is really important. Work out the things that make you unhappy and then ask yourself if there is anything you can do to change those things. If you can change them, then great! But if you can't, just accept it as it is. There's nothing you can do about it, so why worry?

Ask the children to think about the things they do at home or school that build their self-esteem and resilience. Give examples such as working through maths problems, taking part in sports activities or building models.

> **Teaching tip**
>
> In the classroom, make lists of things you can change and things you can't change. Be honest and put things on there that you find frustrating like long queues, slow internet connections and heavy rain when you have no umbrella. Show the children that you have things you can't control that frustrate you and explain that you are going to try and accept these too. This will encourage them to do the same.

3

# Forgiveness

'Why should I forgive people when they are in the wrong?'

**Reflect on what forgiveness looks like and why we should forgive people.**

**Taking it further**

Picture books can be a great source for teaching forgiveness. *I Am Extremely Absolutely Boiling* by Lauren Child, *Will You Forgive Me* by Sally Grindley and Penny Dan or *The Year the Swallows Came Early* by Kathryn Fitzmaurice are all good examples to share with your class.

*It can be hard to forgive people when they have done something that makes us feel sad or angry. When our friends don't want to play the games we want to play, we might get angry. When someone excludes us from their game or activity, we might get upset. That's all part of life. Sometimes we don't want to play a game that a friend wants to play. Sometimes we want to get our own way. When we feel angry, upset or frustrated, the best thing we can do is to take some time out. We need to walk away and realise that it doesn't matter. When others do things that upset us, remember, you don't know the whole story. Maybe someone has just been mean to them. Maybe there's something sad happening at home. Maybe they just need a bit of love from us.*

*If we stay angry at someone, we can start to feel angry at everyone. When we forgive someone, we are expressing kindness, and we feel better. When someone does something that makes you feel sad or angry, take some time out and then forgive them as often as you can.*

Ask the children to remember a time when they forgave somebody. Use these examples with the class as part of a discussion on why forgiveness is important.

# Being wrong

'Is getting it wrong ever right?'

**Show children that being wrong about something isn't an example of failure but rather an opportunity to learn and become more knowledgeable.**

*We are never right all of the time. We don't just get things wrong in maths or spelling tests, we get things wrong with people too. Sometimes we say things that aren't true or sometimes we exaggerate the truth. That's OK. Being right all of the time is boring.*

*The next time a friend says something that you know or think is wrong, don't correct them, ask them why they think that. We can learn new things by listening to others and finding out what they think about things. When we learn things from other people's points of view, it teaches us new things. It might turn out that what we thought is actually wrong.*

*Also, don't be ashamed of changing your mind about things. That's what the mind is for. Think about when you were younger and the things you used to believe then. As we get older, there are lots of new things that we can find out. Our past is full of things we were wrong about.*

*When someone points out that you're wrong, they aren't criticising you, they are trying to learn from you. Tell them why you think certain things and then listen to why they think certain things. That way, we can all learn from each other.*

Ask the children to share a favourite fact. This could be a football statistic, an animal characteristic or a space fact. Then discuss how we can all learn things from each other.

**Teaching tip**

Tell the children about times that you have been wrong in the past. This will encourage them to discuss things that they have been wrong about. That in turn will help the children to understand that we are all wrong about things sometimes and will help them to accept this fully as part of their learning journey.

# First impressions

'They seem like such a nice person!'

**Give children the opportunity to consider what kind of first impression they make.**

The first time we meet someone, we make a judgement about them. 'They seem nice', 'They're very quiet' and 'They're mean' are all first impressions we form after we encounter somebody new. We need to remember that people might be acting a certain way because they feel shy or scared. How we respond to them gives them a first impression of us. Try to make others feel comfortable when you first meet them.

It's perfectly normal to feel nervous when you are in a new situation. Maybe it's the first day back at school after the summer holidays with a new teacher. Maybe it's your first time taking part in a sports club. In those situations, remember that how you make a first impression is important. Be friendly. Smile. Listen to others. Think about what you are going to say before you say it.

You will never get a chance to make a second first impression. When you meet someone new, try to be positive, ask them questions about themselves and pay attention to their answers.

Share with your class an embarrassing, but appropriate, first impression story. Sharing this with your class will show them that we all make first-impression blunders. It will show them that being able to laugh about these situations helps us to know how to deal with similar situations in the future.

**Bonus idea** ★

Create role-play and drama sessions using first impression scenarios. These could be meeting real people such as King Charles III or Grace Darling. The encounters could also be with imaginary characters such as aliens, superheroes or characters in books. These sessions will give the children opportunities to practise how to make their first impression on others a positive experience for all.

# Being positive

'I feel positive today!' said the battery.

**Explore the importance of being aware of negative thoughts and following them up with positive ones.**

*The way that you think about something can be made all the better by thinking about it positively. If we train ourselves to see the positive in different situations, then we are colouring in our lives with positivity.*

*Here are some examples of negative thinking:*

- *I'll never be able to do this.*
- *It's all his fault.*
- *I should have tried harder.*
- *She's doing well. I'll never be as good as her.*
- *I might as well quit.*

*We all think like this sometimes and that's OK. But when you notice yourself having a negative thought, see if you can change it into a positive thought:*

- *I can't do this yet.*
- *I'm in charge of my actions, nobody else.*
- *I did my best. I'll try something new next time.*
- *Everyone is different. I can't compare myself to others because no one else is me.*
- *One step at a time. Every time I do something, I get better at it.*

Another way to help children to focus on the positive rather than the negative is to get them to make a list of things that they are grateful for. This could be friends, family, pets, food, toys, games or something simple, like a rainbow. They can repeat this activity or refer to this list if they're feeling unhappy.

**Taking it further**

Create character names like Captain Fun Popper, Mr Horrible, Nasty Narwhal or Madam Meanstreak. Ask the children to draw these characters and label them with things they might say about others and about themselves.

Then ask the children to create opposite characters, for example, Captain Party Dude, Ms Awesome, Happy Hamster and Madam Lovington. The children now draw and label these characters. This activity will help children to identify the differences between positive and negative thoughts.

# Prepare yourself

'Swallow a toad every morning.' Nicolas Chamfort (Writer)

**Help children accept that things will go wrong.**

*Imagine swallowing a toad each morning for breakfast. Yuck! But imagine if you did start every day like that. Nothing else that happened that day would be as bad as the toad you had for breakfast! This is what Nicolas Chamfort meant by his quote.*

*If we accept that things might go wrong in our day, we're far more likely to react well when it happens. If we expect that, at some point in our day, we might fall over or forget things then when those things happen, we can more easily shrug it off because we were expecting it anyway.*

*It's not being negative, it's being prepared. If we are prepared for things to go wrong, we can react more positively when they do. You trip over? Oh well, everybody does that. A family member shouts at you? Don't shout back. Respond with patience and kindness. And remember, it's better than swallowing a toad every morning!*

Play the game 'Unfortunately, Fortunately'. Before the lesson, prepare some 'Unfortunately' scenario cards. Put them in a bag. Children work in pairs. One child chooses a card from the bag and reads out their 'Unfortunately' statement. Their partner then has to come up with a counter 'Fortunately' statement. For example, 'Unfortunately, the football match was cancelled', 'Fortunately, I got to hang out with my friends instead'.

# Switch off

'Chill out!'

**Encourage children to switch off, unwind and relax to help reduce anxiety and stress.**

*We live in an extremely busy world and are constantly bombarded with noise and information. It's important to sometimes turn off the tablet, phone, laptop, games console or television and try and switch yourself off too.*

*It's great to look forward to things like a holiday, meeting friends or a party but it's also important to think about the present moment. If we stop sometimes, turn everything off and just focus on breathing in and out, it helps us to be present right now. Focusing on a deep breath going in and a deep breath going out helps us to shut off the rest of the world. We don't have to do that for very long but if we practise doing it every day, perhaps before we go to sleep, it helps us to switch off and feel relaxed.*

*You should never feel guilty about switching yourself off sometimes. We all need to do it. It's been proven by clever people like psychiatrists who study the brain. They all agree that switching off your brain and having some 'me time' is absolutely necessary both for your physical and mental health. So, when you are 'just chilling', it means you are working on yourself and making yourself healthier and happier. This 'just chilling' isn't playing a video game or watching a film. That kind of relaxation can be good too but this is different. This is just you, by yourself, taking time out for just you.*

Encourage the children to find a quiet place without distractions at school, home or a place they go regularly where they can just breathe.

**Taking it further**

Make group deep breathing a regular occurrence in your classroom. There are lots of guided breathing meditations for children on YouTube. 'The Mindfulness Teacher' and 'New Horizon' offer short five to ten minute exercises that you can use with your class.

# Be here now

'Just be here now.' Ram Dass (Teacher)

**Teach children to stop and appreciate the now, independently and frequently.**

*We often wish the past was different. We wish we'd scored a goal. We wish we hadn't said something to a friend. But these actions are in the past. There's nothing you can do to change them now. You can learn from these experiences and act differently in the future. But beating yourself up about the past is pointless. Just learn from it and move on.*

*You can hope for something to happen in the future. There's nothing wrong with that. Looking forward to things is good. But the future is never going to happen exactly as you want it to. Things change at the last minute, events get cancelled, people get ill. These are all things that we can't control. The future will never be something that we can control.*

*You can't change the past or control the future. But you can live in the present moment. You can be aware of things you are doing right now. If you are painting a picture, enjoy the colours and shapes that the paintbrush is making. If you are playing in a park, enjoy the smells of being outside and the feel of the wind on your skin. The world is happening right now and you're in it!*

Practise present-moment awareness in your classroom. Set a daily alarm for everyone to stop what they are doing and take a deep breath. Point out the sun shining through the window or the way the sky looks. Find something extraordinary in the ordinary and appreciate it with your class.

# Ego

'Waste no more time arguing about what a good man should be. Be one.' Marcus Aurelius (Roman Emperor)

**Teach children about the inspirational leader Marcus Aurelius and get them thinking about how to live a good life.**

*Marcus Aurelius was a Roman Emperor from the year 161 AD to 180 AD. He was one of the richest and most powerful people in Ancient Rome. Yet he never thought he was better than anyone else and only ever treated everybody he met with respect. He kept a secret diary with advice about how to be the best person he could be. He never wanted this diary to be read by anyone because it was filled with his private thoughts. But when he died, his servants published the diary in twelve books called 'Meditations' and they became very famous across Rome. The books were used as guides for how we can live good lives and are still used like this today by people all over the world.*

*Marcus Aurelius did his best to listen to others to try to learn things from everyone he met. He didn't shout and show off. Try your best to be like Marcus Aurelius and have the smallest ego you can. That's not to say don't be confident and feel proud about your achievements. It's important to recognise when you've done things well. But you don't need to go around telling everyone about how great you are. Live without ego. Live like Marcus Aurelius.*

Ask your class what they would write in a diary giving advice on how to live a good life. Start to collate the ideas and make a group diary with your class adding advice whenever they think of something new. Use the themes from this book to give you ideas.

### Taking it further

Ask your class to research the life of Marcus Aurelius. Get children to ask their family and friends if they know about him and his beliefs on how to live a good life.

11

# Understanding 'bad' people

'Nobody does wrong willingly.' Socrates (Philosopher)

**Examine, using empathy, the choices other people make.**

**Teaching tip**

Online resources from websites such as www. p4c.com (Philosophy for Children) can be a great way to introduce philosophers like Socrates and philosophy to the primary classroom. There are also books such as *Philosophy for Kids* by David A. White, which is also recommended.

*Sometimes, people can be mean to us. But when this happens, try to think about why they did what they did. Something very sad might be happening in another area of their life. It might be that they only said something mean to you because they are sad. So instead of being mean back, try to show them kindness.*

*Of course, if someone is being mean to you all the time, you should talk to a teacher or family member. But if someone you know suddenly starts acting mean, there might be another reason.*

*Reading can help with this. When we read books, we can climb inside the minds of the characters and understand why they make certain choices. Books teach us something called empathy, which means being able to understand and share the feelings of others. Reading makes us better human beings because we're able to understand things from other people's points of view.*

*Unfortunately, we can't do that in the real world so easily, but we can still try to use empathy and understand others.*

*So, the next time someone does something mean, try to show compassion rather than anger. It can be hard to do but the more you try, the better you'll get at it.*

Socrates, the Greek philosopher, has been described as the wisest man that ever lived. Could you and your class find out more about him? What can you learn from his ancient wisdom? What do other philosophers say about empathy?

# Best friends

'You're my BFF!'

**Explore what a healthy friendship looks like and the desirable qualities of a best friend.**

*What makes a best friend? Best friends are meant to be the ones closest to you that will always look out for your best interests. That doesn't mean that best friends never argue. They don't have to agree on everything. They just have to care for each other.*

*If you're spending a lot of time with someone then it is important to know that they are good for you. When you're with somebody a lot, you often behave in the same way that they do. So, if you're with somebody who says mean things about others, you could end up joining in with that same 'gossiping'. But it works the other way too. When you're with nice people, this can rub off on you and you're nice just like them.*

*Ask yourself some questions about your best friends, like:*

- *Do they encourage me to do well?*
- *Are they nice to others?*
- *Do they talk about people behind their backs?*
- *Do I think that they talk about me behind my back?*
- *Are they making me a better person or a worse one?*
- *Should I be spending more or less time with these people?*

*Having best friends is a lovely thing to have. But only if they are the right best friends for you.*

Ask the children in your class to make a list of ingredients that make a perfect best friend.

**Taking it further**

Read *Sharing a Shell* by Julia Donaldson to explore friendship further. This could lead to a classroom discussion on how we help our friends.

**Bonus idea** ★

Create a display in your classroom that encourages children to make positive comments about each other. Set up a 'round', in which each member of the class writes three things that they like about another member of the class. You should assign who writes about who to ensure everyone is written about. Keep it anonymous, then, when children have read their three things, they can guess who wrote them.

# Enjoy your family

'Family matters.'

**Encourage children to be more present at home when spending time with their families.**

Michael Rosen's book *Good Ideas: How to be Your Child's (and Your Own) Best Teacher* is a highly recommended book for the classroom. It was written to be a guide for parents to teach their children fun things at home but it's also a fantastic source of ideas for games in the classroom. Use it to set talking homework to encourage children to be more communicative and collaborative with their learning at home.

*A family sits down together at home. Within a few minutes, somebody has their phone out. A family goes to a restaurant together to share food. Quickly phones and tablets appear, particularly in children's hands, and any conversation is forgotten. Are these familiar situations in your family? Do you grab or get handed a phone or tablet at home or in a restaurant?*

*Technology is a wonderful thing and there's nothing wrong with using it. We can learn lots by playing games and watching videos and have great fun doing it. But, next time you and your family get together, don't reach for a phone or a tablet. Instead, tell your family about your school day. Tell them about the good parts and the bad. Ask them how their day was. Ask them what school was like when they went. Ask them about their favourite teachers, lessons and activities. We often don't realise that we're being so distracted by technology. Don't miss the chance to enjoy spending time with your family – it's important!*

Remind children that their school family is important too. Encourage them to make time to talk with friends, teachers and other school staff as part of their school day. Ask them to chat with lunchtime supervisors, say hello to the school secretary, give a wave to the caretakers and cleaners. Explain that by doing this it makes school a happy and friendly place for everyone.

# You can't get everything you want

'Gratitude turns what we have into enough.' Aesop (Storyteller)

**Examine how to be content with what you already have.**

*Adverts make us want to buy so many things. But sometimes when we get something that we've seen in an advert, it turns out to not be as good as we hoped and we feel disappointed.*

*'Unboxing' or 'First Impression' videos on YouTube show vloggers unwrapping and reviewing products. They give you a chance to look at a product and decide if you really want it. But these videos can also be part of the advertising campaign itself, designed to make you want the product even more. So even though watching these videos is OK, it is important to know that they are trying to make you want more things.*

*We sometimes think that we can have everything we want but that just isn't realistic. It is important to prioritise. Prioritising means deciding which things we really want, and which things we can live without. We can train our minds to ask questions like, 'Do I really need this?', 'Can I make do with not having it?' and 'What will happen if I don't get this thing?'.*

*By prioritising, we are being more realistic about life. It's a way of thinking about what we already have and being satisfied with that.*

Ask your class if they watch unboxing videos. Ask them the reasons why as a prompt to discuss the effect of these videos further.

### Taking it further

Spend a PSHE lesson exploring why unboxing videos can be harmful to children. Ideas to explore can follow the themes of unrealistic expectation and the promotion of both commercialism and materialism. These are big issues and are important discussions to be had in primary school at the appropriate age and level.

# Stories can teach us all we need to know

'Slow and steady wins the race.' Aesop (Storyteller)

**Examine the morals of Aesop's Fables and the valuable lessons they can teach us.**

**Taking it further**

Lots of modern stories have copied the themes of Aesop's Fables and have morals or lessons that we can learn. In *The Gruffalo*, we learn that brains can overcome strength to win the day. *The Lorax* is about the need to care for the planet. *Matilda* teaches us about the power of books and reading. *Elmer* tells us that it's OK to be different and that self-acceptance is important. Can you find more 'teaching stories' to share with your class?

*Aesop's Fables are collected stories, usually about animals, and always about learning lessons. They are said to have been told by the ancient Greek slave and storyteller, Aesop, more than 2,500 years ago. The stories have characters who learn important lessons. The most famous one is probably 'The Tortoise and the Hare', in which a hare makes fun of a tortoise and challenges him to race. The hare is so confident he will win that he takes a nap mid-race, allowing the tortoise to slowly cross the finish line first. The moral of this story is that slow and steady wins the race. These types of lessons are called morals.*

*Other famous Aesop Fables are 'Town Mouse and Country Mouse', where the moral is that it is better to live a peaceful life with few possessions than to live in luxury where it can all end in disaster. In 'The Wolf in Sheep's Clothing', we learn that if we seek to do harm, then harm will come to us. The story of 'The Lion and the Mouse' teaches us that acts of kindness are never wasted.*

*Every fable contains a lesson we can learn. The lessons, or morals, of other Aesop's Fables are:*

- *Never give up*
- *Work hard and play hard*
- *There is always a way*
- *Be a good example to others*
- *Don't underestimate yourself*
- *Learn from failure*

- *Don't always expect to be rewarded*
- *Be happy with what you have*

*These lessons are really important for us to learn so we can have a more positive mindset and a better understanding of what makes us happy. So read more stories to learn so much about yourself and life!*

Set up a recommended reading display of stories with morals. *Tales of Wisdom and Wonder* by Hugh Lupton, *The Pot of Wisdom* by Adwoa Badoe and *The Lion Book of Wisdom Stories* by David Self are great places to start.

**Teaching tip**

Ask children what other lessons they have learned from popular books, such as the Harry Potter or Percy Jackson series. Are there any popular children's films or TV shows that contain morals too?

# Ask for help

'Helping others helps me.'

**Encourage children to ask for help when they need it.**

*Everyone needs help sometimes. But sometimes we feel that we should do everything ourselves. Sometimes we worry that people won't want to help us. Sometimes we think that people will think we're being silly if we ask for help. But it's not true. We all need to ask for help sometimes.*

*But how do you actually ask for help? How do you word it exactly? Do you just say, 'I need help!'? That sounds a bit like an emergency. Here are some ways you can begin asking someone for their help, whether it's a teacher, member of your family, trusted adult or friend:*

- *Can I ask a favour?*
- *Can you give me a hand with this?*
- *What would you do about this?*
- *Could you please help me do something?*
- *Please could you lend me a hand?*
- *What do you think I should do about this?*

*These are some great questions to start with when you need help. Not only does asking for help give you the support you need, it has other benefits too. It can help you become better friends with someone because doing things together can be fun. It also helps you to learn new things about the world, your friends and yourself.*

Give the children in your class examples of when you needed help when you were at school. Then, also tell them about how you ask for help from your colleagues in school now. Show them that you need help as much as anyone else.

# Keep calm and control anger

'Congratulations San Francisco, you've ruined pizza!' Anger (*Inside Out*)

**Explore how children can manage anger and use calming strategies when they feel angry.**

*We all get angry sometimes. It's OK to get angry, but it is important not to let anger take over and control our actions.*

*Abraham Lincoln was president when the United States was split into two parts fighting a war against each other. Lincoln managed to stop this war and brought the country back together. He is remembered today as a person of great character, but even he got angry.*

*Lincoln knew that his anger was not helpful. Anytime he lost his temper, he would sit at his desk and write a long letter to the person that had made him angry. He would explain all the reasons why that person had made him angry. Then he would put the letter into an envelope and put it in his desk drawer. He never actually sent those letters, but writing them helped to make the anger go away.*

*Would writing a letter help you to manage your anger? If not, find a strategy that works for you. For example, you could: count to ten, breathe slowly and deeply, walk away or tell a trusted adult how you feel.*

*Find a way that helps you to take control of anger so it doesn't take control of you.*

Ask children to think about the last time they got angry. What was the reason? Is there anything they could have done differently? What strategy will they use next time?

**Teaching tip**

Exploring how famous people deal with their anger can teach useful lessons to children. From Abraham Lincoln's letter writing to Kendall Jenner's 'Burn Book', there are lots of examples online. Zendaya and Selena Gomez are good role models for how to deal with the 'haters' and not lose yourself to anger. Check out YouTube for examples of how both actors deal with negativity.

**Taking it further**

What other strategies can you use to help children deal with anger? Having a designated area where children can go to calm down both inside the school building and in the playground can help children to manage their anger and also help staff to identify when children are struggling with their emotions.

# Offer to help

'Happy to help!'

**Helping others can be extremely rewarding and increase self-worth, so here we suggest ways that children can help others at school, at home, across their community and in the wider world.**

*Offering to help shows other people that you care about them. They might say no, and that's OK, but at least they know that you're there for them. One form of helping others is by offering encouragement in the things that they do. Telling them 'Well done!' for doing well in a test, scoring a goal or tying their own shoelaces is very pleasing to people.*

*At school, you can offer to help your friends, but you can also offer to help carry things for a teacher, tidy up for the lunchtime supervisors or pick up litter for the cleaners.*

*At home, you could offer to do the washing up, unpack the grocery shopping or take the rubbish out. You could also take some artwork you've made to an elderly care home (with a trusted adult).*

*Help others and feel great!*

Ask the children to identify the things that they're good at. It might be a particular subject in school or it could be something else, like telling jokes and making people laugh. They'll soon realise that you can't be good at everything. We're all different in the things we can do and the things we struggle to do. Remind the children that if they see someone struggling to do something, they can always offer their help.

# Be grateful

'I choose to be grateful.'

**Encourage children to practise gratitude to help them grow into adults that help others.**

*Being grateful isn't just saying thank you when someone gives you something. Gratitude is much more than that. Being grateful is recognising how lucky you are. You're lucky when you have good friends. You're lucky when you're warm and comfortable and healthy because not everybody in the world has those things.*

*When you are given a present and you've said thank you, gratitude doesn't stop there. Ask yourself, what it is that makes you happy about that present? Is there a way you can show how grateful you are? You could write a thank you letter, send them a text or make them a card.*

*Practise gratitude with your family too. You could suggest making a board where people can put up notes saying what they are grateful for. It makes for a great source of conversation.*

Researchers at the University of Nottingham have found that people who practise gratitude are more likely to help others, share, volunteer and donate to charity. How can you incorporate gratitude as a daily practice in your classroom?

A gratitude board is a great idea for the classroom as well as the home. Get children involved in designing the board and deciding where it will go. Leave paper and pens near the board and encourage them to add a note every time something happens that they feel grateful for. A few times a week, get children to read aloud new notes on the board.

### Taking it further

Gratitude can be broken down into four parts:

1. Noticing the things to be grateful for.
2. Thinking about the things you are grateful for in life.
3. Feeling the emotions that those things give you.
4. Expressing how appreciative you feel.

You can regularly apply those four parts to everyday life in the classroom by reminding children to first notice something they could be grateful for and giving them time to think about this before expressing how they feel about it.

# Don't dive in

'Stop, listen and think.'

**Encourage children to pause and think before responding or reacting to others.**

It's all too easy to speak without thinking first. We all do it every day. But if we take our time to think before we say something, it can make a huge difference. Often, we dive straight into our answers with both feet first, but it's so much better to stop, pause and think.

Cato the Younger was a Roman senator who made lots of speeches in public. He was like a celebrity in Roman times and was frequently stopped and asked questions by the press and public in the streets. Before he answered these questions, he always paused and thought for a while. He said, 'I begin to speak only when I'm certain what I'll say isn't better left unsaid.' He always prepared what he was going to say before he said it to make sure that he wasn't going to say anything mean, selfish, rude, arrogant or ignorant. He would only speak if he felt confident his words would do no harm.

Cato's model is a good one for us to follow. The next time somebody says something that makes you feel angry, sad, jealous, embarrassed or any other emotion that needs to be managed, take a breath before you respond. Stop, breathe deeply and think about what you are going to say. If you need to walk away, then do that.

This is something that we can practise with our friends, teachers, family and even strangers. The more you do it, the better you will get. The better you get at it, the smarter you become.

Ask your class to find out more about Cato the Younger.

# Better together

'Together we can do great things.' Mother Teresa (Nun)

**Look at the life of Mother Teresa and see how her inspirational work helping the poor, sick and hungry was spread so much further with the help of others.**

*Mother Teresa was a nun and Head Teacher of a school in India. At that time, a lot of people in India were poor and suffering from illness and hunger. She felt she had to do something, so in 1946 she left her job as a teacher and set up a charity to help. The charity she set up was run by volunteers who gave up their time to build homes, hospitals and orphanages for children who had no parents.*

*Mother Teresa travelled all over the world to make speeches that inspired people to help her achieve her goal. By the time she died, her charity was working in over 100 countries, helping people overcome illness, disease and hunger.*

*Her charity is still going today, being run by volunteers who work as a team. The word 'TEAM' is an acronym for 'Together Everyone Achieves More'. It's true, we can achieve so much more by working together. When we care for each other as part of a team, encourage each other and celebrate success together, we can achieve any goal. We all have individual ideas and strengths, and when we bring them together we are much stronger.*

Set up a whole-school challenge day where classes work together to make music, do maths challenges, or complete outdoor obstacle courses. Afterwards, classes can feed back to the rest of the school in an assembly how they worked together to overcome their own particular challenges.

**Teaching tip**

Tell children: *When Mother Teresa won a special prize for her charity work called the Nobel Peace Prize, a huge party was going to be held in her honour. She asked if the party could be cancelled and the money that it would have cost be given to poor people instead.* Ask the children what their thoughts are about this.

**Bonus idea**

Team games such as scavenger hunts, building towers from mixed materials, LEGO® building challenges, relay races and classroom escape rooms are great ways to help children to work collaboratively.

# Perseverance

'You can do it!'

**Look at how rewarding it feels to persevere and work hard for things like possessions, grades or experiences.**

**Taking it further**

Set perseverance tasks for the children in your class but make sure that some are achievable for all. Search on the internet for 'minute to win it' games as there are hundreds to choose from, then select the ones most appropriate for your year group.

It's the people who work hard to get things that enjoy them the most. If you're given an iPad and you break it, it's very easy to think 'Oh well, I'll just get another one'. But if you work hard at school, save up birthday money, do lots of jobs around the house and finally get that iPad you've worked so hard for, you're more likely to take good care of it.

The word 'perseverance' means that you keep doing something even though it's hard and takes time. Anything you persevere for is worthwhile because working hard teaches you to never give up and to keep on going. Perseverance is impressive. When others see you acting with perseverance, they won't be jealous of you, they will be inspired by you. People don't envy others with perseverance, they admire them.

So, try and have perseverance in all that you do. Persevere when you're at school, playing games, taking part in sports, reading, writing, solving puzzles, climbing a tree, playing a musical instrument, learning a dance move, anything! Always persevere – you'll get better, people will think you're great and you'll feel great too!

Discuss the things you have persevered for in your life. This could be your journey to becoming a teacher or some other worthwhile pursuit that you have achieved.

# Appreciate it now

'It's not what happens to you, but how you react to it that matters.'
Epictetus (Philosopher)

**Examine appreciation as the cognitive act of enjoying something in the present moment, as opposed to gratitude which is more reflective and happens after the event.**

*What do you love doing? Perhaps you enjoy going to the park, cinema, leisure centre, museum, theme park or theatre. What do you do when you're doing something you really enjoy? Are you fully focused on appreciating the fun thing you're doing, or are you thinking about what you're going to do next? Appreciate doing the things you love in the moment and you'll enjoy them even more!*

*Of course, you can't do the things you love all the time. Sometimes you have to sit a test or queue in a long line. Neither of these are likely your favourite things to do, but even in not-so-fun experiences, look around and see if there is something to appreciate. For example, in a test, try to find enjoyment in the challenge. While waiting in a queue, enjoy time chatting to friends or family.*

*Don't spend all week longing for the weekend or you'll miss the fun things that happen during the week. Live in the present moment. Live in the now. Appreciate the now and it makes everything you do more enjoyable.*

Set an alarm at random times of the day. When the alarm rings, ask your class what they appreciate about what they are doing right now. This doesn't need to happen frequently for it to become a habit and your class will appreciate the fun lessons much more.

**Taking it further**

Read your class Eckhart Tolle's book *Milton's Secret* for learning more about appreciating the moment and living in the now.

# Conditional happiness

'I'll be happy on one condition!'

**Explore what psychologists describe as 'conditional happiness'. This is happiness under a particular set of conditions, which means that you are waiting for the right moment or set of circumstances to be happy.**

Ask your class to make a list of the things they are looking forward to in the future. These things might be a holiday, a birthday or something happening at the weekend. Then ask them to make a list, of equal length, of the things that they are happy about right now. These might be related to the weather or something that happened at break time.

Conditional happiness is when you think that you'll only be happy if and when something happens. For example, 'I'll be happy when I have a new phone or games console' or 'I'll be happy when we win this tournament' or 'I'll be happy when we're friends again.'

This kind of thinking is not good for you because if those things don't happen, you feel sad. There's nothing wrong with looking forward to things, but pinning all your happiness on objects, people and events is not a good idea because it leads to more unhappiness.

Happiness can be found right now. You don't need more possessions, more friends, more clothes, more trainers, more success. Those things are very nice and if they do happen, then great! But don't spend your time believing that you won't be happy without them.

Think about the things you are looking forward to. Look forward to them, but not at the expense of your happiness right now. If all you think about is what might happen or what you might get in the future, you're missing what is happening now and what you already have.

Explain and discuss with the children how conditional happiness and real-life happiness just don't go together. You can't find happiness now if you put conditions on your happiness.

# Selflessness

'I love to do things for other people.'

**Examine how we can all be more selfless, with practical ideas to share with family and friends.**

*Being selfless means doing something for other people while expecting nothing in return. There are lots of opportunities for us to help by giving money, such as adopting an endangered animal online, donating to a charity or buying food for someone homeless.*

*But being selfless doesn't have to involve giving your own money. You could tell your family about EasyFundraising, where in return for shopping using links on their website, they make a small donation to your chosen charity. Your family can do their ordinary online shopping via EasyFundraising and donate to a good cause for free!*

*There are lots of opportunities for us to be selfless through small everyday acts, such as holding a door open for somebody, leaving an anonymous kind letter in a library book, or donating a book to a doctor's waiting room.*

*Even though being selfless means that we don't want anything in return for our actions, there is a secret here. Are you ready? The secret is that we actually do get something in return! Being selfless makes us feel great about ourselves.*

Organise a 'selflessness trip' to somewhere in your local community. For example, your class could sing carols at Christmas at an elderly care home. They could visit the local library and run a reading event. You could take them on a litter pick at a local woods or park.

# Doing good

# Part 2

# Choose kindness

'Be kind as often as you can.'

**Give children the opportunity to choose to be kind in any and all situations.**

**Taking it further**

Ask the children to write letters or postcards to a local nursing home. Perhaps even arrange a visit to sing songs there. What other opportunities are there to share kindness in your local community with your class?

*Kindness can be lots of different things. You can do things in school, such as give someone a compliment, use good manners or let someone go in front of you in the line. You can do things at home, such as leave a positive comment on social media, make someone else's bed or make a gift for someone. You can do things outside, such as play with someone who you don't usually play with, offer to tidy up PE and break-time equipment or hold a door open when you go back inside. You can do things that help the environment, such as turning off the tap when brushing your teeth, picking up litter or reusing paper when you are drawing.*

*But perhaps the best way of showing kindness to everyone is to smile at them. Try it. Today. Smile at everyone you meet and, more often than not, you will find that they return the kindness and smile back. If they don't, does it matter? Simply smile at the next person you meet. Soon everyone will be smiling!*

*So today, choose to do something kind. It will make you feel good and make others feel good too. It will also make your family, your teachers and your friends so very proud of you. Let kindness be your choice today.*

Set a kindness homework for the children. They could do something kind for their family such as washing the dishes, making their bed or vacuuming the house without being asked to.

# You are powerful

'With great power comes great responsibility.' Stan Lee (Creator of Spiderman)

**Children discuss superheroes and their powers. Then they are asked to identify what things they could do to be a 'kindness superhero'.**

*You might have a favourite superhero like Wonder Woman, Hulk, Black Widow or Superman. Each one has extraordinary abilities and powers. Superheroes might have different powers but the one thing that they all have in common is that they want to help others. They want to make the world a safer and happier place. Maybe they save people from supervillains, perhaps they stop natural disasters or they might help out animals in some way.*

*Have you ever dreamed of having superpowers? Didn't you know? You already have superpowers! You have the power to be kind, the power to be friendly and the power to help others, just like superheroes do. None of us will ever be able to run as fast as the Flash but you can still use your power for good.*

*You could donate old clothes and toys to charity. You could donate food to food banks or do a sponsored walk to help raise money for a charity.*

*You don't have to find a new superpower. You already have one. Let kindness be your superpower.*

Ask the children to make posters to show off their superpowers. The posters can include suggestions for how others can show their kindness superpowers too. These can be displayed at school or shared at home.

> **Teaching tip**
>
> You and your class could support a charity. You could do some fundraising in school for a local or international charity.
>
> You could also visit the website Free Rice. There is an online quiz on the website that donates a portion of rice for each question that you get right through the World Food Programme, in an attempt to end world hunger.

# Be happy

'Happiness is a choice.'

**Discover the effects smiling and happiness have on our bodies.**

**Taking it further**

Create a class joke book and read a joke a day before the register to have a happy, positive start to the beginning of each day.

When we smile our whole face changes. Our eyes sparkle and our cheeks lift. But something else happens. When we smile, our brain releases chemicals that make us feel good. Clever scientists have discovered that smiling helps us to become calmer and makes us feel happier. So, the best thing to do if you feel sad is smile! That might sound absurd but it really does work.

Smiling doesn't just make you feel better. It makes others feel better too. We all have different parts in our brains. One part is called the 'Reward Centre'. When we win a prize or are given a birthday present, it activates the 'Reward Centre' of our brain and makes us feel happy. When someone smiles at us, this also activates the 'Reward Centre' and makes us happy too. So, when you smile you are making yourself and the person you are smiling at happy too.

**Bonus idea** ★

Read your class *Augustus and His Smile* by Catherine Raynor about a tiger who has lost his smile and goes on a journey of discovery.

Say to children, 'Let's all become happier right now and give each other a great big smile!'. Walk around the classroom smiling at every child and encourage them to do the same. Then challenge them to keep smiling all day to make themselves and everyone around them have a happy day.

# Don't shout

'Raise your words, not your voice. It is rain that grows flowers, not thunder.' Rumi (Poet)

**Explore how shouting doesn't have to be the only solution in an argument, especially if you stop and think first.**

*Shouting is the opposite of smiling. When you shout, negative chemicals are released into your body making you even more angry. When you're angry, you aren't in control. When you aren't in control, you make mistakes. So, shouting means that you are going to make mistakes which you will later regret.*

*If someone says something that you disagree with, you don't have to argue with them. If others don't think the same thing as you, it doesn't really matter, does it? We can all think about things differently and that is what makes us who we are. The world is a wonderful place because we are all different from each other. It never gets boring because it's always interesting to find out what other people think about things.*

*People are not going to agree with what you think all the time. You aren't going to agree with what others think all the time. Even if you don't agree with each other, there is no point in shouting.*

*The next time someone says something that you disagree with, listen to them but don't talk until they've finished speaking. Then think about what they've said. Finally, respond with your opinion but don't react by getting angry about what they say. Listen, think and reply.*

Read *I Really Want to Shout* by Simon Philip with your class and discuss what other strategies they could use when they feel angry.

### Taking it further

Try using instruments such as a singing bowl, ocean drum or energy chimes to make your classroom a calm environment after break and lunchtime. Give the children opportunities to breathe in deeply three times before any words are spoken in the classroom.

# Why worry?

'Don't worry... be happy!'

**Give children suggestions of things they can do when they are worried about something and show them how to identify things they can control and things they can't control.**

*We all worry about things. But most of the time they are things that we can't control. Here are five things we can't control: getting sick, what others say about us, what others think, the weather and past mistakes.*

*We can eat healthy food and exercise to help us not to get sick. We can be kind to others and people may say nice things about us. But in the end, we can't control the outcome. Here are five things we can control: asking for help, who our friends are, taking care of ourselves, how we behave and learning from our mistakes.*

*If you start to feel anxious and worried about something, ask yourself, "Is there anything I can do about this?". If you can't do anything about it, then why worry?*

*If you are worried about things that happened in the past, then remember; what happened yesterday is yesterday. It's what you do today that you can control. Some things are beyond your control and if they are beyond your control then don't worry about them as there is nothing you can do about them.*

Make a list with your class of the things that they can control and the things they can't control and display it in the classroom.

# Love

'Love is a doing word.'

**Look at the power of love and suggest a variety of ways in which children can express their love to family and friends.**

*You can love Netflix, but you need to watch it to love it. You can love playing a sport, but you have to take part in it. Loving something requires participation. It is the same when you love a person. It might be just hanging out and chatting. It might be making them cards or gifts. It might be giving them a hug or a high five. It doesn't matter what it is you do, as long as you do something that shows them that you love them.*

*Another way you can show someone that you love them is through the way you act when you spend time with them. It doesn't have to be anything big; it can be something as small as picking up a dropped pencil for a friend.*

*Just spending time with someone can also show that you love them. You could take a trip to the cinema or even just sit together at lunch. Everything you choose to do with that person shows that you love them.*

*Helping out at home can show your family that you love them. You could help make dinner or do the dishes. It will show that you love and appreciate what they do for you.*

*You don't have to say, 'I love you' to show that you love someone. Show them through your actions and choices.*

Make a list of things that friends can do to show their affection for each other. Make a classroom display with sticky note suggestions.

### Taking it further

Don't wait for Valentine's Day to make cards with your class. Ask the children to make a card for someone they love. It could be a family member, a friend or a pet. Tell them to include a message telling the person or animal how much they appreciate them.

# Face your fears

'Fear is the path to the dark side. Fear leads to anger, anger leads to hate, hate leads to suffering.' Master Yoda (Star Wars character)

**Examine the effects of fear and how we can control it, or even use it, to help us achieve things.**

### Taking it further

Have a PSHE lesson about what the children in your class are scared of. Begin by sharing your own phobias to show that rational and irrational fears are normal. Offer encouragement when a child shares a fear, be patient and show that you take them seriously. Letting children know that they don't need to fear their fear is important.

We are all scared of something. Whether it's heights, spiders or the dark, it's perfectly normal to be scared of things. From learning new sports to looking at maths problems, there are many things that can make us feel scared. The more you do something, the less scary it becomes, but that first time can fill us with fear. The most effective way to deal with fear is to laugh about it. Joke about your fears. When you joke about it, you are talking about it, which helps you realise that everyone feels scared of things.

The army, navy, air force and marines all teach their soldiers to talk about frightening experiences. They know that talking about it makes you feel better. They also train the soldiers to breathe deeply to manage fear. They use different types of meditation, all involving breathing, to calm the soldiers down when they're in difficult situations. So, the next time you feel like something is making you panic, breathe your way through it. Usually, when we get scared, we start taking shorter breaths. Notice when this happens and take long, deep breaths instead. A good technique is to make sure you breathe out longer than you breathe in. Count to three as you breathe in and carry on counting to ten as you breathe out. Then repeat. Simple as that. Just breathe.

The Dark by Lemony Snicket, Little Mouse's Big Book of Fears by Emily Gravett and Levi Pinfold's Black Dog are great books to start discussions about fear.

# I don't know

'Do I need to know everything?'

**Explore the power of not knowing and how to use it as an opportunity to learn new things.**

*Albert Einstein was a really clever inventor and scientist. He taught himself algebra and geometry at a very young age. By the age of 16, he had published his first scientific paper all about magnetism! His theories and ideas have taught us lots about how the universe works.*

*One of Einstein's favourite things to do was to go out onto a lake in a boat with a notebook, lie down and look up at the sky. Once there, he'd think about what he didn't know. Back then, there was no internet to search for the answers to your questions. There were lots of unsolved mysteries. Einstein thought about these mysteries, like gravity, space and time, and came up with theories about them.*

*Einstein was one of the greatest scientists of all time. He believed that it was not knowing something and wanting to know it that led him to his most important discoveries. You should never be embarrassed about not knowing things. So, the next time you answer 'I don't know' to a question like Einstein, make it your business to find out the answer.*

Make a display board where the children can write questions that they want to know the answers to. For about 5 minutes every day, answer some of the questions. It could lead to significant learning because when children go to the effort to write down a question, they must really want to know the answer.

**Taking it further**

Ask your class to find out more about Albert Einstein's discoveries. The 'Kids National Geographic' and 'Britannica Kids' websites have lots of information. But beware, National Geographic states that Einstein was a child prodigy, whilst Britannica says that he did not do well at school! More on this in the next reflection.

# Fake news

'Don't believe everything you read on the internet.' King Henry IX
(Space ninja cowboy from the future)

**Explore the importance of teaching children that not everything on the internet is true.**

When we want to know something, we can search the internet, read books and ask others, but the answer we find isn't always going to be correct. When searching the internet for 'How many cats were on the Titanic?', the following answers were included:

- No cats were on board the Titanic.
- There were cats on the Titanic.
- The ship had an official cat named Jenny.
- Jenny the cat got off the Titanic, taking her kittens with her.
- Jenny and her litter of kittens were on board.
- Jenny the psychic cat predicted the sinking of the Titanic.

So, which one is right? That is something we need to ask ourselves whenever we are learning something new. Not everything on the internet is real or factual.

There is something called 'fake news'. This is where false information is presented as real news. This is done to mislead you into thinking something or buying something. For example, if there was a fake news article claiming that all apples were evil and that we should all only be eating pears... it might be fake news from a company selling pears.

Sometimes people believe what they are posting on the internet is true when it actually is not. This is still fake news as it is being presented as fact when it is not.

*The best thing we can do is look for errors, such as spelling mistakes or images that don't look real. We also need to think about if the website is a trusted source, such as a real news site. Some fake news looks very real but it is important to check a few reliable websites, in case we are being misled.*

*If you're in any doubt, you can ask a trusted adult like a teacher or family member.*

There are relevant resources available on Twinkl, such as differentiated reading comprehensions and quizzes on fake news. Pick one and use it to run a session on how to identify fake news with your class.

**Bonus idea** ★

Send a letter home to families about fake news. This could encourage families to discuss with their children how to spot fake news online. The letter could include information from internetmatters.org (see references).

# Role models

'Who should be my role model?'

**Examine the qualities we look for in a role model.**

The more time we spend with people, or watch and listen to them, the more we say the things they say and act the way they act. We can't help it. It's biological. We learn through imitation, through copying what others do. We start doing this at a very young age and keep doing it our whole lives. So, who we imitate is very important as it makes us who we are.

Who do you look up to and admire? It might be a family member, a friend or somebody you have never even met. It could be a YouTuber, author, TikToker, movie star, footballer, athlete, gamer or illustrator. Whoever it is, think about what it is you admire about them. Is it their ability to do something? Is it the way they look? Is it the things they say?

It's important to think about why you like someone, as the people we choose as role models influence the things we say and do. So, choose somebody wise. Being wise is different from being clever. A clever person might be smart and skilful, but a wise person is patient and has good judgement. A clever person might be able to solve a problem, but a wise person avoids it altogether. A wise person doesn't rush in and knows to stay out of trouble.

Think about your role models. Think about what they do and don't do. What they say and don't say. If they are wise, then choose to follow their example.

Ask the children to work in pairs to identify a role model in their lives. Are they wise? Begin by giving some examples of your role models.

# Mantra

'Mantra! Mantra! Mantra!'

**Explain what a mantra is and how to use it, then get children to create their own.**

*The word 'mantra' originally comes from the Buddhist and Hindu religions. It means a word or sound that is repeated during meditation. These days, mantra also means a statement or slogan that is repeated frequently to keep you calm, centred and focused. Steve Jobs, the founder of Apple, often repeated the mantra 'focus and simplicity' to himself. He did this to remind himself and others what made his company so successful.*

*Mantras can be used to keep you calm in new situations or when you feel overwhelmed. Here are some examples of mantras you could try:*

- *I am not afraid to be wrong.*
- *I support others but ask for help when I need it.*
- *Whatever I do, I give my best.*
- *I have the courage to be myself.*
- *I always learn from my mistakes.*
- *I am ready to seize the opportunities of the day.*
- *I am a good influence on others.*

*What other mantras can you think of?*

Help your class choose their own mantras. Give them sentence starters to help them get started, for example: Today will be _____ , I will always _____ , I will never _____ , I can _____ .

Get them to write their mantras on card and mindfully decorate them. This mindful decorating helps them memorise their mantra.

# Mindful colouring

'Our life is shaped by our mind, for we become what we think.'
Gautama Buddha (Teacher)

**Examine the benefits of mindful colouring, which helps to quieten extraneous thoughts and focus the mind.**

Mindful colouring is when you really pay attention to what you are colouring in. The designs in mindful colouring books and worksheets feature detailed patterns which require you to take your time and really focus. Mindful colouring helps you to stop thinking about what you are going to do tomorrow or what you did yesterday, and instead just think about what you are doing in the present moment. You might be thinking things like 'I will use a green pen to colour the leaves', 'Purple will look good there' or 'The blue background is beautiful'.

Mindful colouring helps you relax and takes your focus off any worries you might have. It's a good idea to do it before you go to bed because it can really help you get to sleep. It helps you slow down and create some quiet space in your mind. It's been proven that just doing 20 minutes of mindful colouring a day can make you calmer and happier.

There's no right or wrong way to mindfully colour. You just do it. Nobody should judge you on your colouring because it's how you choose to express yourself in that moment. It's fun for adults too! It's a great calming and positive activity to do as a family.

Mindful colouring sheets are available for free online. Print off different designs for your class and have them ready for wet break times, golden times, morning activities etc.

# Morning routine

'Carpe Diem!' (meaning 'seize the day') Horace (Roman Poet)

**Explore the benefits of a morning routine that includes some deep breathing.**

*A study has shown that children in primary school need nine to eleven hours sleep a night while teenagers need eight to ten hours sleep. You need more sleep than teenagers so it's important to set sleep goals so that you get enough sleep, are fully rested and can do your best in school. But make sure you get up with enough time to have some breakfast and a moment of peace before school.*

*Create a morning routine that includes some time to relax. When we're relaxed, we learn more and have more fun with our friends. When we're stressed or tired, we can feel grumpy.*

*To give yourself some extra time in the morning, get your clothes ready the night before. That way, in the morning you'll have enough time to brush your teeth, have a wash, get dressed and eat breakfast. Then, before you leave the house, stop and spend a few minutes breathing deeply. A long, deep breath in, counting from one to nine, and then a long deep breath out, counting from nine to one. If that's too long, change it to one to six or even one to three. Three long breaths like that should be enough.*

*Including a few minutes of deep breathing in your morning routine gives you a peaceful moment to start the day. Breathe deeply, just three times then relax and enjoy your day!*

You could also guide children to take three deep breaths straight after registration to help them relax into their day.

### Taking it further

Write a morning routine checklist for your class and give each child a copy to take home and share with their family. Everyone's morning routine will look different, so it's important for children to personalise the list, prioritising what they need to do. Encourage all of them to include the deep breathing, though!

# Bedtime routine

'There is a time for many words and there is also a time for sleep.' Homer (the Ancient Greek author, not the character from *The Simpsons*)

**Look at the benefits of having a healthy bedtime routine.**

*Getting enough sleep is incredibly important for you to be happy and healthy. It's just as important as healthy eating and exercise. When you are sleeping, your brain sorts through the information that you learned that day and stores it. Your brain also replaces chemicals and even solves problems when you sleep.*

*If you don't get enough sleep, you feel groggy and horrible the next day. You become clumsy and forgetful. You can even become ill. Getting enough sleep helps you grow and build up your germ-fighting immune system. Create a bedtime routine that relaxes you and gets you ready to sleep well. Here are some tips for a healthy bedtime routine:*

- *Try and go to bed at the same time every night so that your body gets used to it.*
- *Turn off all electrical devices an hour before bedtime.*
- *Don't exercise just before bedtime as exercise wakes you back up.*
- *Try to make your room as dark as you can.*
- *Reading before you sleep or being read to helps you get to sleep faster.*
- *Try deep breathing before you go to sleep to relax your body and mind.*

Ask children what their bedroom routine is. Can they improve it based on the ideas in this reflection? Get them to try to make changes to their routine and see if it helps them sleep better.

# Elevator breathing

'Breathing slowly calms me down.'

**Practise 'elevator breathing' to get more oxygen into the bloodstream and open capillaries, which helps to keep children calm.**

*We all breathe. But conscious breathing is different to just breathing normally. Conscious breathing is when you pay attention to how you are breathing. Deep conscious breaths help you to relax by slowing down your heart rate. One way of practising conscious breathing is a technique called 'elevator breathing'. Elevators go up and down, and we can imitate this with our breath.*

*To begin, either sit cross legged or in a chair with your feet flat on the floor. Have your back straight and your shoulders back. You can close your eyes if you want to. Check your heartbeat and breathing. Are they fast or slow?*

*Now you're ready to start elevator breathing. First the breath goes in through the nose, down into the chest and then further down into your belly. When you breathe out, it's flipped: belly to chest to nose.*

*The first breath is going to be a really deep one. Breathe in through your nose, push it all the way down into your chest and keep pushing it into your belly. Hold the breath in the belly for a moment then follow the breath back up.*

*Then take another deep breath. Do this ten times in total. You might notice that your heartbeat and breathing have slowed down. This will make you feel all relaxed.*

Children usually only breathe with the top part of their lungs. This technique helps them to use their whole lungs, helping them feel calmer.

**Teaching tip**

Tell children that elevator breathing will probably feel strange at first, but the more they do it the easier it gets. Use this technique when children are angry or stressed, as well as part of a daily meditation.

**Taking it further**

You could start a mindful after-school or lunchtime club which might include more conscious breathing practice. This is good for you both you and the children.

# Train your brain

'Let's work out!'

**Compare the way athletes train their bodies to the way we can train our brains. Build and maintain children's cognitive skills by encouraging them to use their brains to solve puzzles and work out difficult challenges.**

*Professional athletes have to train every day. They have to practise whatever sport they do to train their muscles and prepare for competitions, matches and tournaments. They have to practise specific skills and routines over and over again. That way, they become stronger and more skilled every single day.*

*We need to do this with our brains too. The more we train our brains, the better we get at solving puzzles and problems and working out answers to tricky questions.*

*Brain training can be fun. Jigsaw puzzles, 'I Spy', scavenger hunts both inside and outside, crosswords, word searches, improvisation games, board games, card games and much more are all great for training your brain. Perhaps you could suggest having game nights with your family, where you sit around a table and play together. It's really good for your brain and your family members' brains too.*

**Bonus idea** ★

Michael Rosen's *Book of Play* contains lots of ideas on how to play creatively both indoors and outdoors. Play is great for training our brains and the book shows us how we can have fun while being creative and becoming more resilient.

*When you face challenges in school and think you won't be able to do something, don't see it as a bad thing. See it as something good for your brain. It's the same as facing an opponent in karate, playing against another school in football or competing against a really good netball team. Those are all chances for you to try your best to win. When you face tricky schoolwork, you should look at it in the same way. It's a chance to see how well you've been training your brain. It's a chance to see how clever you are. Don't get frustrated and look for something easier to do, take up the challenge and make your brain the best it can be!*

Collect a box of games for your classroom that will help improve memory and brain training. Charity shops often have these for sale at quite cheap prices.

**Taking it further**

You could set brain training games for homework. You could even ask the children to design their own board games with their families using a template, like the one on this page.

| START | | | | | | | | |
|-------|--|--|--|--|--|--|--|--|
| | | | | | | | | |
| | | | | | | | | |
| | | | | | | | | |
| | | | | | | | | FINISH |

# Practice makes perfect

'Practically perfect? Me???'

**Look at how you can change a habit with training.**

**Taking it further**

You could start, as a class, to practise good habits together. This could be reading more, expressing gratitude, starting a new hobby or choosing something suggested in this book like elevator breathing. Perhaps you could do this at the beginning of each term and discuss at the end of term what worked and what didn't. Being self-reflective as a group is really helpful for growth.

If you perform a dance move ten thousand times, that dance move becomes instinctive. It's all about practice.

This doesn't just happen with physical activities. It also helps when we practise things mentally too. We can train our thoughts, behaviours and reactions to things. For example, we can practise deciding that we won't talk about people behind their backs. We can make the choice not to do it once and then make the same choice again and again and again. The more we do it, the easier it becomes. We are training ourselves to do something unconsciously and instinctively. After a while, we won't even notice that we're making that choice.

We can make a choice about how we react when we become angry about things too, deciding to stop and breathe instead of shout. The more we practise, the better we get.

Take some time to think about what habits you have that you want to change then begin your training. It all starts with that one choice. You could choose to stop talking over other people. You could choose to stop eating unhealthy food. Choose something and begin your training.

Tell your class about a habit that you want to change. It could be spending too much time on your phone or not exercising enough. Tell them that you are going to start your training towards practising better habits. This will encourage them to do the same.

# Structure your day

'Start a daily routine!'

**The school day has a very structured timetable but there are four key points in the day when children can stop, reflect and make their own positive choices within that structure. Help them create a reflection routine.**

*Having a routine is helpful during times of unpredictability and uncertainty. If there are things happening at home making you unhappy, then the predictability and familiarity of the school day can help you. We can all find comfort in the routine and sense of belonging that being part of our school brings.*

*There are four points in the day when you can stop and reflect.*

*In the morning, remind yourself there are things that are in your control and things that are out of your control. If you can't control something, try and put it behind you. Instead, focus on the things that you can control.*

*At lunchtime, remember that you can make your own choices. You can choose to be kind. You can choose to be positive.*

*At home time, reflect on the choices you made during the day. What are you going to choose tomorrow? What will you do differently from today? What will you try and keep the same?*

*At bedtime, remind yourself of all the good things that happened during the day and think about what you are grateful for.*

During the school day, remind children of these four reflection points. After the register, at lunchtime and at home time, give them a few moments to reflect and remind them of what to do in the evening too.

# Having an unstructured day

'Daydreaming is an escape from reality!'

**Studies have shown that daydreaming leads to creativity, innovation and invention. Encourage children to daydream!**

*Our school day is always very busy and our weekends can be filled with visiting family and friends, attending clubs and taking part in activities. But sometimes, after school or at the weekend, it's great to just do nothing. It's even better when you get to 'do nothing' outdoors. Sitting on some grass, looking at the sky, feeling the slight breeze against your skin, smelling the scent of flowers and tasting the fresh air are all fantastic in the spring. As is playing in the snow in winter, kicking through the leaves in autumn and splashing in a paddling pool in summer.*

*When we daydream, we can imagine the future, make decisions about what we are going to do in certain situations and reflect on the past. We can think of happy memories of people and places, and of the things we've done.*

*We can also imagine ourselves as the main character in stories. We can use our imagination to be superheroes, animals or explorers of alien planets. We can create sequels and prequels to books we've read and movies we've seen, and we can put ourselves in the stories! We could be flying side by side with Superman, sailing the seas with Captain Jack Sparrow and swimming with Ariel under the sea. When we daydream, we can go anywhere, meet anyone and do anything!*

Encourage children to spend some time daydreaming in the classroom by giving them some quiet time with calming music.

**Bonus idea** ★

Make 'do nothing and daydream' a reward activity for your class to help them see that doing nothing isn't 'boring' but an opportunity to expand their imaginations.

# Being outdoors

'Born free!'

**When children go outdoors, they refine their advanced motor skills, communication skills, peer relationships and appreciation of the environment. Outdoor play is also directly linked to the development of children's strength, immune system and healthy weight maintenance. Encourage children to get outside.**

*Being outdoors and looking at nature helps us to see how beautiful the world is. Taking time to look at trees and plants connects us with the planet. When we watch animals, we often feel a calming connection with them.*

*When we watch TV, we only have the opportunity to use two senses: sight and hearing. When we're outdoors, all five of our senses are activated. We can feel the weather upon our skin. We can smell wet leaves and sweet flowers. We can taste too. That doesn't mean that we need to lick the bark of a tree, but rather, there are tastes in the air, like the damp taste when it rains. This range of sensory input helps us process information better as we grow up.*

*Being outdoors exposes us to more sunlight, which makes sure we get enough vitamin D to help us grow and makes our muscles and bones stronger. Bright light helps us to concentrate for longer too.*

*So go outside as often as you can. It makes you feel happy and helps you to learn more.*

How can you take more of your lessons outside? Have a set of clipboards ready so you can spontaneously take work outside. It gives an injection of enthusiasm to the lesson, even if it's just for five minutes.

**Teaching tip**

*100 Ideas for Primary Teachers: Outdoor Learning* has lots of activities to make any outdoor space fun and educational for your class.

# Problem solving

'The problem is not the problem. The problem is your attitude about the problem.' Captain Jack Sparrow (*Pirates of the Caribbean*)

**Encourage children to use a four-step approach to solving problems, rather than just giving up, to make them more resilient.**

*Problems are a part of life. Sometimes, when we're faced with a problem, we want to just give up. But problems are opportunities for us to grow. Try to change the way you think about problems. Encourage your class to be problem solvers with a four-step approach:*

1 *Identify what the problem is.*
2 *Develop a solution (or more than one).*
3 *Try out the solutions.*
4 *Ask for help from a trusted adult.*

*When it comes to challenging school work or homework, we can learn how to deal with our emotions by using the four-step approach. For example:*

- *You get a maths problem wrong: ask yourself what have you done in the past that was similar and can you apply those skills to these new problems?*
- *You still get the maths problem wrong: try a new approach to solve the problem.*
- *You still get the maths problem wrong: can you find some help on the internet?*
- *You just can't solve the maths problem: time to ask a friend or trusted adult.*

*The more we try and solve things ourselves, the happier, more confident and more independent we become.*

Encourage the children to play problem-solving games during wet playtimes such as noughts and crosses, board games and building games.

# The power of yes

'Yes! Yes! Yes!'

**Look at what happens when we accept new challenges and new experiences.**

When we find that there's something we like, we usually stick to it. We do it with food, leisure activities and even our opinions. Trying new things like a sport can be scary. Yet saying 'yes' to new experiences gives us opportunities to get smarter and become happier.

If you try something new and it doesn't work out, that's totally fine. Ask yourself, what can you learn from it? What will it be like the second time you try? What will it be like the third time? The twentieth time? The hundredth time? You will get better and better at whatever it is, and you'll have a new skill.

'Yes' is a word that we should use more often. Yes, I will try my best! Yes, I will forgive you! Yes, I will be the best person that I can be.

Saying yes to new things makes us feel less scared and more willing to take risks, creating new opportunities for us to grow into confident and happy people. Sure, we are going to fail sometimes but it's what we can learn from that failure that counts.

Once you get comfortable taking chances, a world of opportunity opens up. Rather than saying, 'I wish I could do that', or 'I wish I was like them', do that thing and be that person. You can be anyone you want to be and can do anything you want to do!

To emphasise the power and frequency we say 'yes', play the 'make me say yes' game in class, where you ask a pupil questions but they aren't allowed to say 'yes' as a response.

## Teaching tip

What new experiences have you taken on recently that you could share with your class? Demonstrating your own growth mindset is essential for modelling to children that we all need new experiences and challenges.

## Taking it further

Read Carol Dweck's book *Mindset: The New Psychology of Success* to learn about how to help children move from a fixed mindset to a growth mindset.

# The power of no

'No! No! No!'

**Look at the reasons why children should sometimes say no to things and demonstrate how children can say no politely and kindly.**

*Sometimes we get asked to do things we don't want to do. Sometimes we have no choice but to do them. But there are occasions when it is OK to say no. You can say no to unnecessary things like keeping up with all the TV shows on Netflix. Our friends might like reading certain types of books or playing certain games. That's OK, but you don't have to like the same things. For example, if a friend asks you to watch a spooky film with them but you know that you won't like it, it's OK to say no.*

*Saying no isn't rude when you say it in the right way. Be firm but polite. Here are some examples:*

- *I just can't, I'm sorry.*
- *Sadly, I have other plans.*
- *I'm busy that day.*
- *Thanks for asking but I can't.*
- *I've already got so much to do.*
- *Maybe next time!*
- *No, thank you, but it sounds great.*
- *I know you like it but it's just not for me.*

*Saying yes opens the door to new and exciting experiences but if you're only saying yes to please other people then it might be worth considering saying no instead. Saying no can help you feel less worried and overloaded. You need to try new things, but you don't need to do everything! Prioritise what you want to do and say no to the things that you don't.*

Give the children examples of when you have said no to things that have been positive to you.

# Failure vs success

'It does not matter how slowly you go as long as you do not stop.'
Confucius (Chinese Philosopher)

**To encourage a growth mindset, children need to learn how to fail. Examine how failure and success are intertwined.**

*Failure is part of the journey towards success. You need to fail in order to succeed. Each failure is a stepping-stone towards success.*

*Actors, musicians, authors, artists, athletes and other famous people who are successful will know failure very well. Talk to any successful person and every single one of them will tell you the same thing. Their success was only achieved by failing many times along the way. This is known as the iceberg of success. An iceberg is a great metaphor for success because icebergs are much bigger below the surface than they are above. What we see is the tip of the iceberg floating on the surface of the sea. This represents success. But hidden below the surface is a huge body of ice. This represents the hard work, doubts, criticism and most of all, failure, that is hidden behind every success.*

*We all fail at times. How we act after we fail is what is important. We need to get back up and keep on going if we want to be successful. Failure and success are all part of the same wheel going round and round together. They are totally linked. So, the next time you fail, know that you are on the road to success. Unsuccessful people give up after their first try. Successful people accept failure as part of the journey. What will you do?*

Revisit the topic of a growth mindset with your class and discuss the benefits of being someone who tries hard in all they do, no matter how many times they fail.

**Teaching tip**

Read James Nottingham's book *The Learning Pit* and explore which resources you can use with your class to help them use failure to reach success.

# Living the good life

'Do the right thing!'

**Examine the Buddhist model of the eight-fold path in the context of modern living, and how children can apply it to their own lives without needing to be religious.**

**Taking it further**

You can apply choosing the right action to your classroom and school rules. Look at each rule and explain why this is the right action. Ask the children what right action they might do for each rule. For example, if you have 'Don't hurt others' as a rule, the children could suggest things that they *should do* instead, like 'Always help others' or 'Always act with kindness'. If you have a rule like 'Work hard and allow others to do the same', then children could suggest what they *shouldn't do,* like 'Don't distract others' or 'Don't give up easily'.

In the Buddhist religion, there is something called the eight-fold path. These eight parts are:

- *Belief – faith in the religion*
- *Resolve – determination to follow the religion*
- *Speech – to speak only the truth*
- *Action – to do only good things*
- *Livelihood – to earn a living doing good*
- *Effort – to put all your energy into living well*
- *Thought – to consider only good things*
- *Meditation – the practice of concentration*

*You don't have to be religious to live like this though. We can all work on these eight areas and do the right thing. If we don't hurt others, don't steal and don't do things we know are wrong, then we are living a good life. When we choose to do the right thing, we are on the path to a happy life.*

*Be the person you want to be. Show the world who you are through your actions. Show them, don't tell them. Choose the 'right action'. If you choose to do good, you are going to have a good day.*

Tell your class about examples of when people have been kind to you in your life both at work and at home. Then ask them to share examples.

# Choice

# Part 3

# Silence

'Silence is a source of great strength.' Lao Tzu (Philosopher)

**Look at the benefits of remaining silent and letting others speak.**

### Teaching tip

In drama lessons, use mime activities such as 'mirroring' where the children take turns to copy each other's movements in silence. This helps to make silence with others seem more normal.

*Ask yourself: are you better at talking about yourself or listening to others? It's easy to talk about ourselves because we know all about the things that we've done. Therefore, it's far more interesting to find out about other people. When the person you are having a conversation with is talking, try to be as silent as possible. Nod and smile, but be silent. Be sure they have finished talking before you start. Make sure that they feel heard. When they want you to speak, then of course you should. Tell them why you agree with something they've said or let them know that you have done the same or similar things. This is how strong friendships are formed. It's the silence and listening that help make these friendships special.*

*Sometimes it's hard to be quiet when you're bursting with things to say! You can practise being silent when you're doing breathing exercises. It can be hard to focus when you're in a busy house or school, so you could use ear defenders and noise-cancelling headphones. After some practice though, they might not be necessary; you might be able to block out the sound by simply focusing on your breathing. Counting while breathing also helps to shift your focus from the things around you to just counting and breathing. The more you practise, the better you get.*

Practise silence in the classroom when reading, doing assessments and practising breathing techniques. Use a singing bowl to focus children and signal the start and end of the silence, or use a singing bowl YouTube video.

# IDEA 52

# Climb a tree

'To climb a tree is for a child to discover a new world.' Frederick Froebel (Educator)

**Look at the benefits of supervised tree climbing and teach children how to climb a tree safely.**

*Climbing trees can be exciting and fun, while also helping us connect with nature. It's also great for our physical and mental health, but it's really important to follow the tree-climbing safety rules. Let's take a look at what they are.*

*Wear shoes that have good grip on the soles, for example, walking boots. Some trainers have slippery soles, so don't wear those. Avoid boots that are too big, like wellies. Crocs, sandals, shoes with a heel and flip-flops are also definitely out!*

*Pick a dry day to climb a tree. Trees are slippery when wet, which makes it easier for you to fall. Find a tree with lots of low branches. Test the branches to make sure they don't snap easily. Make sure you push down on a branch to ensure it is strong before stepping on it.*

*Go slowly, even if you feel confident and remember to have three points of contact with the tree at all times. That means if you want to move your arm then your other arm must be holding a solid branch and both legs must be on something solid too.*

*When you climb back down, take the same route that you took up.*

*And the most important rule of all is only climb a tree with a trusted adult present.*

Always consult the Senior Leadership Team of your school before allowing any child to climb a tree, even under the appropriate supervision.

### Taking it further

The website 'The Conversation' has an interesting article in which five experts, including a paediatric surgeon, are asked if children should climb trees. They all agreed that children should be given the opportunity to climb trees for many reasons including building their confidence, developing their physical strength and developing a growth mindset. Have a read and see if you agree.

# New beginnings

'A new start is a new opportunity.'

**Share five tips for how children can use the opportunity of a new week, day or lesson to change their mindset and start afresh.**

**Taking it further**

Educator Brenda Dyck shares her own story and advice about offering pupils fresh starts on EducationWorld.com. You can find the link in the references.

*Schools are a great place for fresh starts. You might have made mistakes in the past but that's where you can leave them; in the past.*

*It's all about how you think about things. Instead of thinking, 'Here we go again', try thinking, 'Great, a new start!'. That might sound easier said than done. What you need to remember is that it's never too late to change and make a fresh start.*

*There are only five steps needed to change your mindset and create a new beginning:*

1 *Accept what has happened in the past and decide you want to move on from it.*
2 *Decide that you are going to get stuck in and do your best from now on.*
3 *Accept feeling anxious and nervous – that's normal.*
4 *Take a long, deep breath and tell yourself that you can do this because you are amazing!*
5 *Smile and be yourself.*

*You are an individual and there is no one else exactly the same as you in the world. So be the best version of yourself. If you need a new beginning to do that then take the opportunity for a fresh start today.*

At the beginning and end of each day, remind those who perhaps need reminding that the day ahead or the next day is the opportunity for a fresh start. Do this as positively as possible and smile!

# Be a seeker

'Seek it and find it.'

**Reflect on the things that children might seek to improve about themselves and learn a breathing technique known as 'box breathing', or 'square breathing'.**

*To 'seek' something is to look for something. Seekers are those Quidditch players who have to find and catch the Golden Snitch in Harry Potter. We can be 'seekers' too; not in the world of Harry Potter, but in this one! We can seek to improve ourselves in some way. It might be that you are seeking to become better at science, art or music. You might be seeking to become better at cricket, rugby or tennis. You can also seek to become a happier and calmer person. You can even seek to be more like your real self and less like others.*

*Box breathing can help with this. Box breathing is where you breathe in for four seconds. Hold your breath for four seconds. Breathe out for four seconds. Pause for four seconds, then start again.*

*While box breathing, think about what you are seeking in life.*

*Box breathing helps you focus your mind on what you really want out of life, and also reduces worry and makes you feel calm.*

Do some box breathing as a whole class. First, get children to think about something they are seeking to change. Then ask them all to find a comfortable seated position and close their eyes. Guide children by counting out loud to begin with, then tell them to carry on breathing and counting in their heads for a few minutes. After the exercise, ask children how it felt to box breathe.

**Taking it further**

Doing any of the breathing exercises mentioned in this book for just 5 minutes a day helps children to feel more relaxed. It's a great routine for every primary classroom to practise. Choose some of the suggestions and see if you can fit in one a day.

# When others do you wrong

'Deal with the faults of others as gently as your own.' Chinese Proverb.

**Revisit the power of forgiveness and forgiving ourselves.**

*There are times when others will say things that hurt our feelings. You can choose to react like this: "What do you know about it?" or "Who asked you?" or "It's none of your business!" or "Go away!".*

*But, if you respond in an angry way, the situation usually gets worse. The best thing to do is be calm, patient and understanding.*

*Sometimes people get bad tempered and become grumpy. If people are grumpy, give them some space. If they say things and do things that are hurtful, do your best to walk away. As you walk away, consider times you have been bad tempered and grumpy in the past. You will have done or said things that will have hurt others, even if you didn't mean to.*

*The first step towards forgiving others is to realise that you have been at fault at times in the past. But be gentle with yourself. It's OK that you have been at fault. Then apply that same gentleness to others. They are at fault right now and that's OK too. Forgive them.*

*Forgive yourself and forgive others as often as you can.*

Rachel Bright's picture books deal with themes such as forgiveness, like *The Squirrels Who Squabbled* and *The Whale Who Wanted More*. Picture books like these are a great way to begin class discussions about big topics.

# Talk to others

'Sharing joy is double joy and sharing sorrow is half sorrow.' Swedish Proverb.

**Look at the benefits of children talking to trusted adults about their concerns and worries and review when to share happy news.**

*When we feel scared, sad or worried, it's a good idea to talk to a friend or trusted adult. Sharing our concerns helps us deal with them. It also helps develop a strong relationship with the person we talk to because, after the conversation, they know and understand us a bit better.*

*Sometimes when we're worried, our natural instinct is to go quiet and not speak to anyone, but that will only make things worse. Decide who you trust the most at home and school. Choose someone you feel comfortable with. It's a good idea to choose that person before you need their help.*

*When we're happy, we want to tell everyone all about what has made us so happy. Maybe we've got a new pet, are going on a special holiday or have received an amazing birthday present. Remember though, there is a time and place to share good news. If a friend has just told you that they are feeling sad, or you know that they are having a difficult time, then don't start talking about your good news. Choose a time and place to share happy news by thinking about the feelings of others.*

*If you have happy news to share with the class, make sure it is at an appropriate time such as a 'Show and Tell' or 'News' time.*

*Not Your Typical Dragon* by Dan Bar-el helps children see that it is important to be yourself but sometimes we need to choose the right time to do certain things.

**Taking it further**

*The Huge Bag of Worries* by Virginia Ironside is another great book for helping children see how important it is to talk about their problems.

63

# Build your confidence

'Try it or you'll never know!'

**Examine the positive effect trying something new has on our confidence.**

When was the last time you did something new? How did you feel? Doing something new can be exciting but also a bit scary. It's worth doing though, because doing something new builds our confidence.

The new thing could be trying out a new sport, getting a new haircut, making an origami model or starting a band with your friends. All these things build your confidence as you learn new things and realise you can do something you couldn't do before!

You could do something that feels familiar first, and then try something new. For example, you could watch your favourite movie with a family member or friend, and then watch a favourite movie of theirs that you have never seen.

Whatever new thing you do, make sure you tell yourself how amazing you are after doing it. You could go to a mirror and tell yourself there. It's a great way to build self-confidence. You could even open your bedroom window and shout out to the world how amazing you are. Go on, I dare you to do that!

Doing new things makes us feel better about ourselves. So, what are you going to do today?

Get children to think of something new they could try. Share a list of after-school and lunch clubs available to your children to inspire them further.

# Brain building

'Train your brain.'

**We look at how we can train our minds to become strong like we can train our bodies.**

*Martial arts, military training, athletic training and many other types of training rely on something called 'muscle memory'. This is where you do something over and over again so that it becomes instinctive. Your body has done it so often that it just knows what to do when you need it to. Musicians who play instruments rely on muscle memory so that they can just play the instrument and let the music flow through them; their body just knows what to do to make beautiful sounds.*

*We can do this with our brains too. We can train our brains to react in certain ways when we practise over and over again. Practise forgiveness, kindness, being calm and being slow to anger. Practise not letting things bother you. Train your mind to cope with these things over and over again. After a while, you won't need to practise as your mind just knows how to react to any situation. Practice and training make your brain strong. It makes you strong.*

*When bad things happen, you can just say to yourself, 'This is what I've been training for! I can cope with this! Bring it on!'.*

Place posters around the school with quotes that promote strong mental health. For example: 'Only you get to control your reactions', 'You are powerful', 'Choose to embrace life', 'Stay cool and calm', 'You are strong'. They might just help the right child at the right time.

## Teaching tip

This might be a useful lesson when teaching too. Remember, the boxer who has never been punched will panic in the ring. Take the punches along with the victories in the classroom. It all makes you a better teacher.

# Praise yourself

'Am I really the greatest in the world?'

**We look at what effects 'over praising' has on children's self-esteem. We also examine how children can praise themselves when they have done something well and boost their own confidence without the need for external praise.**

**Teaching tip**

Over praising also lowers the bar on expectation. If children don't try very hard at something and we tell them that they are doing a fantastic job then why would they need to push themselves any further? We are teaching them that to try a little and to do mediocre is all they ever need to do.

Their confidence will come from doing and trying, from failing then doing and trying again. Resilience leads to confidence and over praising stops this from developing.

*There are times when we hear grown-ups tell us we have done well at something, but they just go over the top. 'That's the best idea in the whole entire world!', 'That is the most amazing thing I have ever seen in my life!' or 'You are the greatest artist in the universe!'. Heaping praise upon us can feel good at first but then you begin to think it doesn't feel real or true.*

*But when we hear 'That's a good idea', or 'That's great' or 'You did a lovely piece of artwork', then know that this grown-up is being genuine. That praise is really true. They mean it and you should feel proud of yourself.*

*You should also feel proud when you do something and you aren't praised for it. When you've done something well, don't be afraid to praise yourself for it. You know when you've done well in sports, gaming, work in the classroom or something else. Tell yourself you are proud. Tell yourself you are happy with your achievements. Don't expect to be praised all of the time by others when you can do it yourself. Also, you'll know that your own praise is real and genuine.*

Children absolutely know when they are being over praised. If we tell a child who has spelt a word incorrectly that they are doing an amazing job, this teaches that child that praise is not always accurate. We can encourage them to try again but over praising them does more harm than good.

# The war within

'Control yourself!'

## Examine self-control.

*There is nothing wrong with feeling any emotion. It is perfectly normal and natural to feel all kinds of different emotions throughout our day. Sometimes we have all these emotions inside of us that we think we can't control. Like in the movie 'Inside Out', it feels like we are being controlled by our joy, anger, disgust, fear or sadness. But the truth is that we can control our emotions. We can fight them! We are the commanding officers in the war within ourselves.*

*You shouldn't feel like you have to fight your emotions, but if you want to then you can. Strong emotions aren't bad. They might mean that you are embracing life. But if you want to fight your emotions, just know that all you are doing is trying to control them, you aren't getting rid of them forever.*

*To control your emotions, take in a deep, long breath. Then identify what the emotion is. Then see if you can identify what could be making you feel this way. Is it a person or situation? Is there a better way you can cope with it? Should you accept it? Should you say something? Should you walk away?*

*You can be in charge of your emotions. You can choose to fight them. But remember to choose your battles carefully. Sometimes accepting you feel this way is the best course of action.*

You could connect this reflection to your school behaviour policy or class charter, for example, the colours on the Zones of Regulation could be referred to.

### Teaching tip

Can you share with your class a time that you controlled your emotions? It could be a story from when you went to school or when you controlled your fear and overcame something. Showing that you, as a positive role model, can do it will encourage the children to do the same.

# Character

'Character cannot be developed in ease and quiet.' Helen Keller (Activist)

**Look at the life of Helen Keller and reflect on the importance of showing your character through your words and actions.**

**Taking it further**

Do you have Young Carers in your school who are children that take care of family members at home? How can their actions, and the actions of other children like them, be celebrated in school?

*When Helen Keller was a toddler in 1882, she lost her sight and hearing due to an illness. Her teacher, Anne Sullivan, taught her how to read using Braille, a reading system for the blind. Anne also taught Helen to speak. Helen went on to give talks all over America and across the rest of the world. Helen wrote lots of books about her and Anne's lives and became a very influential activist, author and educator on how to treat those with disabilities.*

*The work of Helen Keller is still remembered and influential today. Through her actions, she showed the world that she would let nothing stop her making positive changes.*

*What can you do to show people your character? It's not the clothes you wear or how many friends you have that show people your character. It's your words and your actions that make up your character.*

*True success isn't having the highest number of social media followers or more money than everyone else. True success is having a strong character revealed through your words and actions. True success is being happy with what you are doing and who you are.*

You and your class could find out more about the life and work of Helen Keller. The *Little People, Big Dreams* series of books by Maria Isabel Sanchez Vergara are fantastic for teaching about inspirational people.

# Focus on your choices

'Wrong is wrong, even if everyone is doing it. Right is right, even if no one is doing it.' William Penn (Writer and Missionary)

**Examine how to make reasoned choices.**

*Things often happen that are beyond our control. A bus we are riding might break down. Severe weather might mean that our school is closed. There is nothing we can do to stop these things from happening. The only thing we have control over is how we react to them.*

*When we react, we make a choice, and we should make a 'reasoned choice'. A reasoned choice is one we've thought about. When we really think about a choice and make our decision based on what we think is the best for everyone, including ourselves, and what we think will do the most good, then we have made a reasoned choice.*

*Whatever happens to you today, try to make reasoned choices. Rather than rushing in and making a quick choice, stop, think and consider your options before you make a final choice.*

*It's all too easy to think, 'What will I get out of this?' or 'Will I be rewarded?'. Reasoned choice isn't about looking for rewards or only focussing on what is best for you but rather what is best for everyone.*

Most children show an understanding of perceived 'right' and 'wrong' from a young age. Whenever you are reading a class text, use the opportunity to ask *why* the characters are behaving in certain ways. Ask the children what they would do. This helps teach valuable reading comprehension skills but also reinforces the concept of reasoned choice.

### Taking it further

Reasoned choice is linked to reasoning skills as they are both ways of thinking about how you think. There are good resources on Twinkl that help children understand how to use these skills which will help them to make reasoned choices.

# The joy of walking

'I love to walk to school.'

**Look at and celebrate the many benefits of walking and talking.**

As well as all the benefits of walking mentioned in the reflection, a walk provides plenty of learning opportunities. Teach the geography and history of your local area outdoors as often as you can.

**Taking it further**

Consider delivering a PE lesson as a long walk outside, with appropriate adult supervision, in your local area.

*When did you last go for a walk outside? A walk in the park, on the beach or in the woods? Walking is a great way to connect with nature, discover new places and have new experiences.*

*Walking also has all kinds of benefits for our bodies, both physically and mentally. Walking outdoors can improve our mood and make us feel better. It makes us stronger, healthier and it improves our flexibility, balancing skills and sleep.*

*Walking with our family and friends is great as it's something that we can do for free, helps us develop road safety awareness and it's good for the planet as we're not making more pollution, which we would be if we got a lift in a car. It can be fun, too!*

*A walk with a family member or a friend is a good opportunity to talk about things too. Sometimes it can be more difficult to talk about a problem face to face. When you are walking side by side, there is limited eye contact which can make it easier to share your worries. Being outside often helps you to feel calm and happy, which helps you to see that perhaps what you were worried about isn't all that bad after all.*

*Take a walk outside for 20 minutes every day and you'll feel great!*

Take your class for a walk in your local area. Tell them to use all five senses while they are outside. What can they see, hear, smell, feel and taste? Ask them how they feel before and after the walk.

# Weeds are flowers too

'Everything has beauty, but not everyone sees it.' Confucius (Philosopher)

**Help boost children's self-esteem using a metaphor about the equality of weeds and flowers.**

*Sometimes we think of ourselves as outsiders. We think we don't quite belong or fit in. We think of ourselves as different to other people. We feel like we are weeds growing in a garden of flowers. But do you know what the difference between a weed and a flower is? Nothing!*

*All weeds are just flowers. You might see yourself as an outsider, as a weed, but it's not true. You are equal to everybody else. We are all equal. We all have the same worth. Think about daisies and buttercups; they are called weeds but they are just as beautiful as daffodils and tulips.*

*Be yourself. Be beautiful like the yellow dandelion and golden buttercup. It doesn't matter who you are, just be yourself. Be like the wildflowers, radiating beauty and just being themselves, not caring whether people think they are a weed or not.*

*So, if you ever feel like an outsider and think you don't fit in, remember the weeds and wildflowers and just be yourself. Grow with confidence wherever you are and be beautiful.*

To reinforce the figurative language of the reflection, sow a pot of wildflower seeds inside the classroom in late March or outside from April to June. Read the label and follow the instructions for full details. As the flowers sprout and grow, read the reflection again. Consider the beauty and variety of what emerges.

### Taking it further

Show the children images and brief descriptions of wildflowers. For example: 'Daisy: Likes the sunshine and grows only 10cm tall. Small white and yellow flowers that grow well with others. A must for a wild and beautiful lawn.' Or 'Thistle: Tall and prefers the shade. Purple flower that dominates the garden. Has protective spikes and a deadly sting.'

Ask the children to choose which wildflower they think they are most like, based on the picture and description. Then ask them to explain why. This activity will help you get to know the children in your class a bit better and gives you an insight into how they see themselves.

# Everything changes

'Every season changes and so do we.'

**Take inspiration from nature to see how change can be a good thing, and examine the role of change within all of our lives.**

**Taking it further**

Look at other examples of change in nature, such as the metamorphosis of the butterfly, dragonfly and frog. Use these as examples of how we can all make changes to become the versions of ourselves that we always wanted to be.

*In the winter, some trees lose their leaves. These trees are called deciduous trees. They change each season, growing leaves in the spring, bursting with health and vitality in the summer, turning orange, yellow and red in the autumn, before fading to brown and losing their leaves in the winter... only to grow all over again in spring.*

*Other trees, called evergreens, stay the same all year round. They endure the wind, snow and rain and always stay the same. They don't seem concerned with how cold it gets. They stand their ground and patiently wait for the seasons to change.*

*People are like trees. Some people seem to be constantly growing and changing their appearance. Some people change their minds about things all of the time. Sometimes people want to be our friend and other times they don't. These people are like the deciduous trees.*

*Other people seem to be the same every time we meet them. They keep the same hairstyle and wear the same clothes. They are always in the same mood and seem unchanged no matter what happens. These people are like evergreen trees.*

*Which type of tree is it better to be like? Which type of tree are you?*

*It's best to be like both.*

*Be like the deciduous trees. Be adaptable and strong when change happens. Make the best of each situation and keep challenging yourself to accept the change that is out of your control.*

*Be like the evergreen trees. Don't expect things to always go your way. Be patient when things are not going well for you, for better times are coming. Stand your ground and wait for the change that always comes.*

Observe the changes in nature over the year and remind children about this meditation and how they can be deciduous, evergreen or both, depending on what is happening in their lives.

# Changing our minds

'Progress is impossible without change; and those who cannot change their minds cannot change anything.' George Bernard Shaw (Playwright)

**Look at what happens when we change our minds and how it leads to having a growth mindset.**

**Taking it further**

Ask your children to find out more about the Stoic philosophers like Epictetus.

We all wish for things to be different at some point, even when we get what we want. We want things, get them, and then don't want them anymore or get bored of them or grow out of them. We change our minds. Other people change their minds too. It's a big circle of change that we all experience.

The Ancient Greek philosopher, Epictetus, was criticised for changing his mind about things by the other philosophers of his time. But he always said that of course he was going to change his mind; that was what the mind was for! You should learn new things and adapt your thinking constantly. Epictetus saw this as a very good thing. He said that if the mind was fixed and closed, there would be no gaps for new ideas to get in. He saw changing your mind as the sign of someone with great intelligence.

Don't be afraid to change your mind. Learn from books, documentaries, websites, your teachers and other people. Listen to different viewpoints and then decide for yourself what you think. And don't worry if you have a different opinion from someone else. We're all different and that's what makes us who we are. Be a person who can grow by changing your mind about things through learning.

Play the game 'Would You Rather' with your class to show how we all have different opinions about things. This might change their minds about what they think of certain things.

# Why care about what others think?

'Are they talking about me?'

**Explore how we respond to what other people think about us.**

*We can all be affected by what other people think or say about us. If we buy a new pair of trainers that we think look great, but our friends say they don't like them, we might start thinking differently about the trainers. We might even never wear them again. Why? Why do we so easily change our minds?*

*We can control our own opinions, but we can't control other people's opinions. So why change our opinion just because others don't agree? If we like wearing certain clothes, then who cares what others think about them?*

*Don't live for the approval of others, otherwise, you'll be waiting a long time to fully live your life. You can't have everybody's approval all of the time. You can't please everyone, so stop worrying about it. Stop caring what others think about you. Just be yourself.*

You can reinforce this with three activities:

1 Integrate self-reflection at the end of the school day to foster a positive self-image. What am I grateful for today?
2 Teach children about different cultures, traditions and religions to show them how diverse our world is, and what a better place it is because of that diversity.
3 Reinforce the message that there are things we can and can't control. Help them to focus on the things that are in their control.

**Taking it further**

Read *The Boy Who Would Be King* by Ryan Holiday which looks at the life of the Roman Emperor Marcus Aurelius. The book contains strong messages on how to deal with what others say about us.

# Small steps

'The journey of a thousand miles begins with one step.' Lao Tzu
(Chinese Philosopher)

**Teach children how to break goals down into small steps to help
them start to do so independently.**

*If you want to reach a goal, such as being a
great goalkeeper or learning a dance routine, it
can be hard to know where to start. Every goal
starts with one small step.*

*You have to learn how to catch a ball before
you can be a goalkeeper. You have to learn
separate steps before you put them together
into a routine. Any goal is only achieved by
taking these small steps, one at a time.*

*It's the same with 'self-goals' too. If you aim to
be happy, friendly, kind or caring, you have to
take small steps towards these goals too. In this
case, you might make small individual choices
each day, like being positive, working hard,
being modest and telling the truth.*

*Alternatively, your 'self-goal' might be to not
react angrily when you can't do something.
Work out the small steps towards your goal. In
this case, step one might be to notice when you
get angry and breathe instead of shouting. Walk
away and calm down. It might not work at first,
step two is to try again. The more you try, the
better you will get at it, and soon you'll reach
your self-goal.*

Get children to identify a goal they want to
achieve, and then tell them to make a plan for
achieving it. Reinforce this triadic approach:

1 Break the goal down into small steps.
2 Track your progress.
3 Modify the steps as necessary.

# Be one with the trees

'Trees are poems that earth writes upon the sky.' Khalil Gibran (Poet)

**Look at the symbiotic relationship between us and trees, and share ideas for how children can enjoy and celebrate trees.**

*Trees are vital for our survival on planet Earth. We breathe in oxygen; trees add oxygen to the atmosphere. We breathe out carbon dioxide, a gas that is harmful to the planet; trees remove this carbon dioxide by absorbing it into their leaves. We breathe in what the trees make, and they take in what we breathe out. A perfect partnership.*

*Trees are also important because we make medicine from them, eat their fruit and use their wood to build things. Trees are really important. Treat them kindly and enjoy them! Here are some ways how.*

*We can use fallen branches and leaves to build shelters or dens. We can make collages and other textured art with sticks and bracken. We can do maths activities like measuring the height of a tree using our own footsteps, a trundle wheel and tape. We can work out the age of a tree using something called 'Mitchell's rule' using only a leaf identification sheet, tape measure and calculator.*

*When we touch a tree, we connect with nature. Try feeling a tree blindfolded; it'll really help you to appreciate the texture and the scents that the tree produces. Show the trees how much we appreciate them. Go on, give a tree a hug! It feels great!*

Are there any trees on your school grounds? Get children to find out more about Mitchell's rule and find out their ages. Do some of the activities in the reflection with trees at your school or in your local area.

**Taking it further**

Ask children if they can think of any other ways of connecting with nature in your school ground or in your local area.

# Cleanliness

'Wash your hands!'

**Examine the reasons why it is essential for our physical and mental health to keep ourselves and the space we live in clean.**

**Taking it further**

The NHS have Activities of Daily Living (ADLs) in the form of handouts and information leaflets on topics like hygiene for children. Try and get hold of a class set to send home to reinforce this important message for children.

*We all know it's important to wash our hands regularly. When we wash our hands, we are killing germs to stop us getting sick. It's also super important to clean our teeth. By doing so we prevent toothache, tooth decay and bad breath, keep our gums healthy and make our teeth look bright and sparkling. Washing our bodies and hair is also important to get rid of body odour. These actions, along with wearing clean clothes, all make us feel fresh and ready to go. This gives us confidence and sets us up for the day ahead.*

*Scientists also think it's important to keep the space around you clean. They say when there's mess all around us, it negatively affects our mood and ability to function properly. So, keeping your room at home clean and tidy is important as well.*

*If you need help tidying your room, ask your family. You could begin by saying:*

- *I know you're busy, but...*
- *Later on, can you...*
- *Please could you help me with...*
- *I just need a little help with...*

*If you share a room, keep it tidy together.*

*So, remember, keep yourself, and the place you live, clean and tidy to be the best possible you!*

Try to link this message with Health Education teaching during PSHE lessons appropriate to your year group.

# Hope

'In the long run, the sharpest weapon of all is a kind and gentle spirit.'
Anne Frank (Diarist)

**Look at Anne Frank's inspirational diary and life story, and explore how she found hope among despair.**

*Anne Frank's diary is world famous. Anne was a Jewish girl who lived in Amsterdam in the Netherlands during World War II. She was forced into hiding with her family when the Nazis occupied the Netherlands. We know that all people should be treated equally but sadly the Nazis didn't believe this. The Nazis wanted all Jewish people to be killed. They invaded lots of countries and took control. So, Anne and her family hid in a secret place above her father's work. They could only get to it by crawling behind a bookcase. It was in this place that she wrote her diary.*

*This diary inspires people to be kinder to each other. In her diary she wrote, 'Footsteps in the house, the private office, the kitchen, then... on the staircase. All sounds of breathing stopped, eight hearts pounded... Then we heard a can fall, and the footsteps receded. We were out of danger, so far!'*

*It is a tragic and exciting account of real bravery in extraordinary circumstances and can teach us about the power of hope. The diary describes the hatred and violence of the Nazis and their leader, Adolf Hitler. But Anne also describes the love, kindness and gentleness of her family and others like hers. It is there that she found hope in the despair.*

The focus of Anne Frank's diary is on hope. Allow time in the classroom for further discussion on this subject.

## Taking it further

The picture book by Jeff Gottesfeld *The Tree in the Courtyard* is the perfect introduction for children to Anne Frank's story. It is told from the perspective of a horse chestnut tree and is beautifully written and illustrated.

# Community

'We are stronger together.'

**Reflect on what it means to be part of a community and review the communities that the children are part of.**

The word 'community' means a group of people living in the same place or a group of people that have similar views or interests. So, your neighbours and the people who live near you are your local community. Your school community is all the staff and children at your school.

Being part of any community means having access to help when we need it, but it also means that we should help others too. Stone Age communities relied on each other to share the work they needed to do to survive. Some people went hunting, some gathered fruit and nuts, some gathered wood, some went fishing, some were lookouts for dangerous animals, some built and tended to fires, some prepared the food. Everybody was involved and the work was equally divided. Everybody contributed something to the community.

We still need to contribute to the communities that we are in today. School communities work together to learn and have fun. Local communities look out for each other and offer help where they can. Members of online communities contribute opinions, theories and ideas.

If we are knowledgeable about something, we can share this knowledge with others. Being in a community is a strength because we are all stronger together than by ourselves.

Discuss your local community with your class. Brainstorm the places they can visit with their family such as the park or community centre.

# Choose words carefully

'Be nice!'

---

**Examine the effect words can have on others, including on social media and the long-term implications they could have on our future selves.**

---

*Our words are powerful tools and we need to be careful how we use them. Our words can heal or hurt, or do good or bad. We need to think about our words before using them.*

*Communication is how you speak, write or use other mediums such as texts, emails or tweets to express yourself. Careful thought is necessary so that we don't hurt others' feelings with our words.*

*Careful thought is also needed when communicating online. Even though you can't physically see the person you're communicating with, they will still get upset if you write something mean. Also, when you get older and go for job interviews, your employers may look at your online profile. If they see that you've sent mean messages online, then they may not give you the job. Employers would worry that you might speak to people in the same way in the workplace.*

*Everybody checks your online profile as you get older. So be careful what you say both online and in person as it might affect your future self! Always communicate kindly to people.*

Although the legal age for children to be on many social media platforms is 13, the reality is that many children have accounts at a much younger age, therefore helping children to stay safe online is important. You could use this reflection to start a conversation about what experience children have with social media.

**Taking it further**

There are websites that outline the danger of what you say online. Kidshealth.org has more on this. You can find the links in the references.

# Show mercy

'I forgive you.'

**Examine what it means to be merciful, taking an example of a time when Winston Churchill showed mercy.**

**Taking it further**

Find out more about Winston Churchill in the *Horribly Famous* book by Alan Macdonald.

*Winston Churchill was the leader of the UK government who led Britain to victory during World War II. Before that, Winston Churchill visited New York. While crossing the road, he was hit by a car. Luckily, he survived but was taken to hospital with his injuries.*

*The driver of the car that hit him went to visit Churchill in hospital to say sorry. Churchill accepted the apology and told the man he understood it had just been an accident. Churchill asked the man what he did for a living. The man replied that he was currently out of work. Churchill offered the man some money to live on while he looked for work. Winston Churchill showed mercy to the man.*

*Mercy is when we show compassion and forgiveness towards someone when we could have them punished. Churchill could have had the man arrested, but he didn't. He was merciful.*

*The man that hit Churchill with his car only did so accidentally. If someone spills something on us or breaks our toy, usually these are just accidents too. Of course, if someone does these things to us deliberately, then we should tell an adult. But if it was accidental, we should show mercy, forgive them and move on.*

Discuss the difference between things that happen accidentally and things that happen on purpose so your class clearly understand how and when to be merciful.

# 7 steps forward

'I keep taking one step forward and three steps back!'

**Look at a 7-step approach to dealing with things positively.**

1) Don't fight the change. Change happens. Try to accept it.

2) Remember that change is just a process that we all have to go through.

3) Think about why you might be scared of this change. You could write down what it is you are scared of or worried about. Writing about feelings can really help you feel better.

4) Try to look at the positives that might come about from the change. Are there any good things that could happen?

5) Think about other times when you have dealt with change successfully. Remember how you dealt with those times. Can you do that again?

6) Try to breathe deeply and relax as often as you can. This helps us to deal with any stressful situations.

7) You may not be able to control what happens in life but you can choose how you want to react to things. Try to remain calm and ask for help if you need to.

Remind the children in your class who they can talk to if they are worried about anything. They could talk to you or a colleague if they need to.

**Taking it further**

Make time to discuss changes in children's lives. Help these children by following these 7 steps:

1. Advise the family to give the child as much time as possible to prepare for the change. Advance warning gives time for processing.

2. Make time to listen to the child and their family.

3. Give the child access to books about the life changes.

4. Keep routines for the child at home and school as consistent as possible.

5. Reassure the child that school will stay the same even if home might be changing.

6. Make sure the child feels like they still have choices at home and school.

7. Talk about other changes that the child has coped with in the past.

# Life lessons

Part 4

# The phoenix

'From out of the ashes...'

**Use the myth of the phoenix as an example of how to overcome disasters.**

*Sometimes disasters happen. Homes flood, pets die, family members move to other places. When these things happen, we can feel powerless. We often begin to wonder why these things have happened, but the fact is that they just do. We can do nothing other than accept it.*

*The word crisis means 'a time of intense difficulty'. In China, the word for crisis is 'Wei-Ji'. The exact translation of this word is 'danger and opportunity'. In all crises, there is an opportunity. There is always something we can gain from the experience. It might not feel like it at the time but getting through each crisis makes us stronger.*

*The phoenix is a mythical bird that lives for around 500 years then bursts into flames and burns to grey ashes. From these ashes, it is reborn into a brand-new form and lives again.*

*During difficult times, will you remain as ash or rise up like a phoenix?*

*When you accept a crisis, you are becoming a bright and shining phoenix that has been reborn through the fire of adversity. Shine on and be an inspiration to others.*

Read the children a Firebird story such as 'The Bennu Bird' from *Pyramids and Pussycats* by yours truly. Discuss how the children can be like the phoenix and shine brightly through their words and actions.

# Professor X

'The greatest power on Earth is the magnificent power we all of us possess; the power is the human brain!' Professor X (Leader of the X-Men)

**Examine the power of our own decision making and how we can make the decision to do good in life.**

*Professor X is a fictional character from Marvel's X-Men. He is a mutant with superhuman abilities. He has telepathic powers and can move things with his mind. He can also read people's minds and control the minds of others, making them do things that he wants them to do. In real life, there is nobody like Professor X. We control our own minds; nobody can make us do anything we don't want to do unless we let them. You have a choice. It's up to you how you behave. It's up to you to be the person you want to be.*

*Professor X can make people forget things. He can wipe memories. Fortunately, we keep our memories, and it is the memories of our failures and our successes that we can learn from. Making mistakes is part of life and it is how we grow as individuals. But for that growth to be worthwhile, we need to make good decisions. We need to choose to do good as often as we can.*

*The next time you make the wrong choice, just remember that nobody made you do it. It wasn't Professor X controlling your mind. You did it, so learn from that mistake and move on.*

Tell children that doing the right thing is habitual. Help the children in your class form this good habit by reminding them of the four reasons for doing the right thing (see the Teaching Tip).

**Teaching tip**

The four reasons for doing the right things are: 1) Character: always choose to be the 'good character' in your life story. Remember that you are the hero! 2) Trust: trust others often. The more you do this, the more people will trust you. 3) Endearment: people will like you when you do the right thing. 4) Teacher: be a teacher to others by showing them how to act. When you do the right thing, it teaches others to do the same.

# Fire and water

'This too will pass.' Persian Proverb

**Look at how every situation, no matter how bad, always changes.**

*No matter how difficult a situation might be, it will change. Nothing can carry on forever. Just as fire always burns out, situations always change. The bushfires in Australia, the wildfires in Southern California and the Great Fire of London all eventually burned themselves out. Firefighters did their best to help of course. King Charles II himself rolled up his sleeves to throw leather buckets of water onto the fire in London in 1666. Just as he helped his country, people will help us too. There are always people who can comfort us when we need assistance through difficult situations. Our teachers, friends and family can all help us get through these bad times but knowing that the bad times will get better can offer some comfort too.*

*Water always finds its level. A wild and stormy ocean eventually becomes calm. This is the same in life. There is balance. There are good times and bad. That's not to say that while the good times are happening you should be expecting the bad to come. Enjoy the good times and love every minute. But during the bad times, wait it out knowing the good times are on their way. Wise people are patient people. It might take some time, but it will be worth it.*

*So, the next time you find yourself in a bad situation, take the help that is offered or ask for the help you need. But also know that fire burns out and water finds its level. All things change and this too shall pass.*

Try to encourage children who are going through challenging times to take some solace in knowing that this too will pass.

# Dance

'Just dance!'

**Look at the positive physical effects that dancing has, including cardio fitness, improved flexibility and increased strength.**

*Dancing can be great fun. Whether it is dancing with friends at school, around the kitchen with our family or solo at the park with headphones in, it's very good for our bodies and minds.*

*When we dance, we are learning new skills and training our bodies. We are improving our balance, flexibility and posture. We are increasing our strength, agility and stamina. Dance also teaches us how to exercise safely and look after our bodies. It is an excellent way to develop well-rounded and full-body physical fitness to improve the condition of the body. It's good for our hearts and lungs.*

*Dance isn't just great for our bodies, it's great for our minds too. It gives us confidence and boosts our self-esteem; it makes us feel fantastic about ourselves! If you join a dancing club, you're also part of a team and can make new friends. Dancing helps you to get creative when you make up your own new moves. It makes you resilient, meaning that you don't give up easily. It makes you a determined person who achieves your goals!*

*When you have finished dancing, whether it's as part of a competition or a five-minute dance in your living room, you feel a sense of accomplishment. You stand, walk and compose yourself much more confidently when you dance often. So, dance whenever and wherever you can!*

Tell all your children to get up – because you are going to dance together!

### Taking it further

Is there a dance club in your school? If not, then you could start one! Advertise any dance clubs in your local area and encourage the children in your class to join.

### Bonus idea ★

Get your children dancing for a few minutes after lunch every day. It helps diminish feelings of lethargy and puts them in a positive mood to learn.

# Criticism

'There is only one way to avoid criticism; do nothing, say nothing and be nothing.' Aristotle (Philosopher)

**Review different types of criticism and how to respond to it.**

Criticism can be difficult to take. When people criticise our appearance, what we say or what we do, we can feel hurt. Sometimes the people criticising us don't realise that they are being hurtful, but even so, it doesn't feel very nice.

There are two types of criticism; constructive and destructive. Constructive criticism is when someone is trying to help you. You might have got something wrong and they are pointing it out. Or maybe they are trying to help you get better at something. Destructive criticism is someone choosing to be unpleasant or nasty.

The best thing to do the next time anyone criticises you is to follow these six steps:

1 Remain as calm as you can.
2 Pay attention. If it's constructive criticism, what they're saying might be useful.
3 Ask questions to find out why you are being criticised.
4 Don't criticise back.
5 Find a solution to the problem that the person criticising you has.
6 Reflect and learn from the experience.

When you receive criticism, follow these six steps, then choose to listen to it, do something or ignore it. The power is in your hands!

Review the two types of criticism with children. Ask them what type of criticism your feedback is. Reiterate that your feedback is constructive criticism when returning work to them.

# Wisdom through science

'Wisdom is the daughter of experience.' Leonardo Da Vinci (Polymath)

**Look at the life of Leonardo Da Vinci and learn about the scientific method.**

*Leonardo Da Vinci was an artist, sculptor, engineer, writer, scientist, anatomist, botanist, composer, musician and inventor in Italy in the 15th century. Phew! He was a very busy man. He was born in 1452 and died in 1519. He painted the Mona Lisa, probably the most famous painting in the world, designed helicopters and discovered new information about how the human body works.*

*Leonardo used something called the 'scientific method' to discover and invent things. The scientific method follows this line of thought:*

1 *Ask a question. What do you want to know?*
2 *Gather information and observe.*
3 *Try to guess the answer.*
4 *Experiment and test your guess.*
5 *Analyse your test results. Were you right or wrong?*
6 *Try another guess if you were wrong.*
7 *Present a conclusion. What have you found?*
8 *Retest again to check the results.*

*Leonardo followed these eight steps whether he was building a flying machine, making a musical instrument, or working out how blood flows through our bodies. He really was amazing, and the scientific method was one of the keys to his success. Why not give it a go!*

Learn more about the life and work of Leonardo Da Vinci in the *Little Guide to Great Lives* series by Isabel Thomas.

**Teaching tip**

Encourage the children to follow the eight-step scientific method not only in science experiments, but in other subjects too. They could, for example, use the eight steps to find out which colours can be combined to make other colours in an art lesson. The more they use the method, the more they will use it instinctively both at school and at home.

# Experience

'By three methods we may learn wisdom. First, by reflection, which is noblest. Second, by imitation, which is easiest. Third, by experience, which is the bitterest.' Confucius (Philosopher)

**Look at how our experiences teach us valuable lessons.**

**Taking it further**

Encourage children to find out more about the philosopher Confucius. The Kiddle.com website is a good place to start. You can find the link in the references. They could also read *Who Was Confucius?* by Michael Burgan.

*If we were told what sand felt like but never touched it ourselves, we would only have a partial understanding of what it feels like. If we touch sand, we experience how it feels for ourselves. This is how we learn best. Experiences are a great way for us to learn new things. But, in today's quote, the Chinese philosopher Confucius said that experience is bitter. What did he mean by that?*

*Confucius says in order to become wise, we should reflect on things, which means thinking about them. Next, we should imitate others, which means copying them. For example, you might copy the way a family member acts when meeting new people. You imitate people and behaviours that you look up to. After that, Confucius says that we should go out and experience the world. He says this can be bitter because not everything in life runs smoothly. For example, you want to run faster. First, you think about running faster, then you watch your friends to see how they run fast, then you try running fast for the first time and fall over. This is the bitter experience! However, if you get up and do it again, you'll get better at running. We are less likely to fall over again because we learn from the first experience.*

Tell the children that by reflecting, imitating and experiencing the world, they will learn better and become wiser. Ask them to try these steps out on something that they want to improve on.

# Be a sponge

'With imagination you can be anything you want to be.' SpongeBob SquarePants (Sponge that lives in a pineapple under the sea)

**Look at how children can filter out the information they don't need and absorb the things they do need.**

*We receive new information every day from our phones, family, friends, teachers, TV and YouTube. It would be impossible to remember all this information. The things you are taught in school are very important. So, listening and trying to remember everything there is top of the list. Listening to your family is important too. But trying to remember everything you've heard online would be impossible. Also, some of the information there might not be true.*

*The yellow, square sponge known as SpongeBob is based on a real aquatic animal whose body is full of pores and channels that allow water to flow through them. Cells then filter food from the water that is pumped around the body and back out again. This water flows in and out with the sponge only keeping exactly what it needs to survive.*

*We need to be like this creature. Not like SpongeBob, who cries for 20 minutes after stubbing his toe, but like the marine creatures who take everything in but only keep the things they need. But this doesn't just apply to information. Let joy, acceptance, gratitude and love be the things that you keep inside. Let all the negativity go and absorb only happiness.*

Link this idea to a breathing exercise. Tell children to breathe deeply in and out. Tell them to imagine breathing in love, happiness, and joy on the inhale, and to imagine breathing out anger, pride or negativity on the exhale.

**Taking it further**

Watch a YouTube video of a sponge feeding underwater with your class. Remind them of this example of letting good things stay within and letting the bad things go. Observe other examples of this flow in nature, such as the tide going in and out.

# Be a bee

'We're like bees in a hive.'

**Examine how we are all part of a global family. Compare humans to bees, working together in our world hive.**

Read your class the picture book *If the World Were a Village* by David J Smith. This book breaks down the staggering numbers of world population to just 100. For example, if the world were a village with 100 people in it, 61 villagers would be Asian (of that, 20 would be Chinese and 17 would be Indian), 14 would be African, 11 would be European, 9 would be Latin or South American and 5 would be North American.

The book goes on to compare languages, ages, religions, food, health etc. It's a great way to help children understand the global community and its inequality.

The population of the UK are descended from many ethnic groups. These include the pre-Celts, Celts, Romans, Anglo Saxons, Vikings and Normans. Since the 15th and 16th centuries, there has also been lots of immigration into our country from Africa and the Caribbean. The British Asian population also has a long history, dating back to the 17th century. The UK is a huge mix of culture, traditions and history, and it has been that way for a very long time.

In an earlier reflection, we looked at the life of Marcus Aurelius. He was one of the first writers to discuss 'cosmopolitanism' which means that we are all part of one world family. The Roman emperor considered himself not just a citizen of Rome but also a citizen of the world. He tried to make decisions that would benefit everyone. In his books, he wrote, 'That which isn't good for the hive, isn't good for the bee.'

At the beginning of 2022, the UK population was 65,110,000. That's a lot of people! If we all live life following the right action, considering each other's feelings, expressing gratitude for what we have and doing the right thing, then this country will be a happy hive of bees who all work together. Be like the bee and choose goodness with wise actions. Then we'll all be in this happy hive of acceptance, tolerance and celebration.

Teach children about how bees work together in a beehive. Compare your school to a beehive with everyone working collaboratively to help each other.

# Adversity

'Resilience in the face of adversity.'

**Teach children a technique to use when they face adversity to help them better deal with it and accept it.**

*Adversity means a difficult situation. From the moment we are born there is adversity. As babies, we got hungry and tired. As toddlers, we had to learn how to communicate, which was frustrating at times. As we got older and started school, we had to learn how to build relationships with other children and adults. Today, we may encounter problems with friends and family. Whenever we meet adversity, it can be useful to S.T.O.P. This means:*

*S. is for Stop. Just stop. Whatever you are doing and wherever you are, just pause for a moment.*

*T. is for Take a breath. Breathe in deeply.*

*O. is for Observation. Observe what is happening and do your best to accept it.*

*P. is for Process and Proceed. Once you have noticed that this is an adverse situation, consider if there is anything you can do about it. If you can make a change then do. If you can't, then there's nothing you can do, so just accept and move on.*

*Try to S.T.O.P. every time you face adversity. This might sound simple, but it's not always easy to do. Sometimes walking slowly can help. Move your body slowly and deliberately as you breathe. Try your best to move on from what has happened.*

You could have a tray or box of pebbles for the children to use when carrying out S.T.O.P. They could hold one whilst meditating, to help them focus. This is called object meditation.

**Teaching tip**

Display the acronym S.T.O.P. in your classroom to remind children to remain calm and follow the four steps when adversity strikes.

# Riddles

'Riddle me this, Batman.' The Riddler (Supervillain)

**Look at how solving riddles is a good exercise for our brains.**

**Taking it further**

Begin a book of class riddles compiled from riddles written or found at home plus ones written in the classroom. Riddles help strengthen children's language skills and enhance linguistic awareness. Plus, they're fun too!

*Riddles are often written in the first person and the past tense. They are deliberately phrased so that the person answering has to use ingenuity to solve them.*

*Riddles can be about anything. Animals, weather, food, objects, you name it, there can be a riddle about it. Here are three famous riddles:*

1 *What gets wet while drying? A towel.*
2 *What belongs to you, but others use it more than you do? Your name.*
3 *It happens once in a year, twice in a week, but never in a day. What is it? The letter e.*

*Riddles are a great way to practise solving problems. They encourage us to be creative and use our critical thinking skills. They make our brain work but in a fun way! They can make us laugh too. Laughter has been proven to relax the brain and body, making us feel good.*

*This is a riddle from 'The Hobbit'. The character Gollum asks Bilbo Baggins to guess what he is describing:*

*'Voiceless it cries,*
*Wingless flutters,*
*Toothless bites,*
*Mouthless mutters.'*

*Can you guess the answer to this riddle?*

Ask the children to solve the riddle. (The answer is the wind). Find some more riddles for children to solve, and get them to try writing one of their own.

# Pinwheels

'Thought is the wind, knowledge the sail and mankind the vessel.'
Augustus Hare (Writer)

**Make pinwheels and do three different breathing exercises.**

*Paper windmills or pinwheels are really easy to make. You can download free templates on the internet. You could ask someone in your family to make one with you. You could print it in your local library or ask your teacher for help. You'll also need scissors, a straw and a pin.*

*Once you have made your pinwheel, go outside and see if the wind will make it turn. If it's too windy, the pinwheel will break. If it's not windy enough, nothing happens.*

*You can also make the pinwheel turn using your breath. Try using three different breathing exercises to make the pinwheel turn.*

1 *Breathe normally to make the pinwheel turn. Do this for one minute.*
2 *For a second minute, use short and fast breaths to make the pinwheel turn quickly.*
3 *Finally, use deep, long breathing for one minute to make the pinwheel turn. Repeat these three steps three times.*

*How did the three different breaths make you feel? Practise your favourite breathing technique. You could blow on dandelion seeds, make a sheet of paper flutter or make a feather twirl.*

Make pinwheels in class and practise the three breathing techniques. You can print the pinwheel template on A3 paper so that your class make giant pinwheels.

**Taking it further**

If you do print out a pinwheel or windmill template for your class, try and find one with a mindful colouring pattern on it. That way, when the children decorate it, they are doing so in a mindful way, making them calm and happy.

# Slavery

'Slavery and freedom cannot exist together.' Ernestine Rose
(Suffragist)

**Look at the life of Olaudah Equiano, an enslaved person who
became a writer to educate the world about his experiences.**

## Teaching tip

Read your class
*Olaudah Equiano: From
Slavery to Freedom*
by David Thomas.
This is a child-friendly
account of Olaudah's
life and contains lots of
information on the topic
of slavery which can be
used as discussion points.

*Slavery is when one person owns another
person. The enslaved person has to work and
receives no money or appreciation. We could
use the example of Cinderella; she had to work
for her step-sisters and got no money, so we
could say that she was a fictional enslaved
person. However, slavery is not fiction. It is real.
Sadly, it is part of our history in the UK. Enslaved
people worked in terrible conditions just to
make other people's lives more comfortable.
Lots of African people were taken from their
homes and enslaved by people from the UK and
other European countries. Ships travelled from
Europe to Africa, where people were either
kidnapped to sell or trade for goods. Some
enslaved people were taken to the Caribbean to
work on farms and in rich people's homes. This
journey was known as 'The Middle Passage'
and went in a triangular shape. Other enslaved
people were put on ships and transported to
the Americas. These enslaved people then
worked to produce tobacco, cotton and sugar,
which was taken back to Europe and sold for
lots of money. The ships were terrible places
for the enslaved people, as they were packed
in horrible conditions. They suffered greatly on
the journey, and if they survived, they suffered
even more greatly where they worked. These
enslaved people were not treated as human
beings and it was all for money.*

*Olaudah Equiano and his sister were kidnapped
from their homes in Nigeria. They were
separated as they were taken to ships and never*

*saw each other again. Olaudah was taken to the West Indies, where his British enslavers sold him. He was only ten years old.*

*Olaudah experienced many terrible things but was eventually freed. He then travelled to the UK, where he wrote a book about his life story. This book became very famous and taught people about what it was like to live as an enslaved person. This book helped towards slavery being abolished.*

*Olaudah took his awful experiences and did something positive with them. He wanted to use his suffering to stop the suffering of others. He was an inspirational man that we can all learn from today.*

There are Twinkl resources supporting the teaching of slavery with sensitivity for EY to KS2 and beyond. Choose one and use it as a follow-up activity to this reflection.

### Taking it further

The Black Curriculum website has resources that support educators teaching Black British History, including information on slavery.

# What are you worth?

'I'm so worth it!'

**Look at how children see themselves and their own self-worth.**

*If I had a £5 note in my hand right now, how many people would want it? What if it was a £10 note? Or a £20 note? OK, but what if I screwed it up? They are all made from plastic, so they are pretty tough. Hands up if you would still like it.*

*What if I threw it on the floor and stamped on it? Hands up if you would still like it. It's plastic, so it's a tough material. The £20 note would still be OK. It might need a wipe down but it would be OK. Well, unfortunately, I don't have a £20 note so you can't have it. Sorry about that.*

*But what I would like you to remember is that message. You all still wanted the money even though it had been crumpled up and stood on. It was still money and was still valuable. No matter what happened to it, it kept its worth and its value.*

*You are worth much more than £20. You are more valuable than any amount of money. But when bad things happen to you, much like they happened to that £20 note, you straighten yourself out. You can wipe yourself clean and start again. I don't mean you literally get crumpled up and stood on. I hope that doesn't happen to you! I mean when bad things happen in life, like you fall over, people are mean to you or you make mistakes, you still hold your worth and you still hold your value.*

*We are tough like plastic. We are valuable like money. You are worth everything in this world.*

Perform this reflection using real or fake money to solidify the message and the metaphor.

# A reaction or a feeling?

'Like fragile ice anger passes away in time.' Ovid (Roman poet)

**Run an activity with ice cubes to help children understand the difference between a reaction and a feeling.**

*Take an ice cube in one hand. You can put your fingers around it or just hold it in your palm. Don't drop it. Try to keep it in one hand. How do you feel? Is it uncomfortable? Take a few deep breaths. Just breathe your way through. Any difficulty or discomfort will pass.*

*We're going to wait one minute. How do you feel now? Is it more difficult to hold the ice in your hand or less?*

*Now you can pass the ice back and forth between your hands. How does it feel? When the ice has completely melted, take a deep breath and dry your hands.*

*If you didn't drop the ice, well done! If you didn't pass it to your other hand until the end, then a big well done too. You might have felt uncomfortable and found the exercise difficult. But the important thing is that you didn't react to those feelings.*

*Having feelings is important and natural. But it is how we react to those feelings that is even more important. Try not to react straight away when you have a strong feeling like anger or sadness. Instead, do what you did with the ice. The feelings will pass. Just breathe through. Let the feelings melt away.*

Repeat this experiment to give the children who dropped their ice or passed it between their hands too soon another go.

### Teaching tip

Make sure that there is enough ice for everyone and that this activity takes place somewhere where the ice can melt to the floor. Paper towels will be needed for the children too. Remind children frequently about the exercise to allow them to practise not reacting to feelings straight away.

# Observation

'Keep on watching.'

**Children look at an object and observe every detail while doing a breathing exercise for relaxation.**

*If we look at an object like a lit candle, a seashell or a flower, we might notice things like colour and shape. If we observe those same objects, we take in much more detail.*

*You can watch TV or YouTube. But if you observe something, you are really watching it. You aren't distracted by your phone or tablet or other people. You concentrate on just watching something. We can try this out as a class or in small groups or partners. You can also do this by yourself at home in a quiet place.*

*Sit up with a straight back and relax your body. Whatever the object is, be it a candle at the front of your classroom, a large seashell on a desk or a flower in your hand, look at it carefully. Notice every shade of colour. Look at the different shapes and lines. Go deeper into your observation. Focus only on the object. Try to block out any sounds or movements around you. Just be aware of the object and nothing else. Then breathe deeply.*

*Perhaps the candle will flicker, the shell might reflect light or the flower might turn in your hand, just accept the object for what it is. Just breathe and observe. Try not to let anything distract you. There is just you and the object.*

*After two minutes or more, bring your attention back to the present moment. Take a deep breath in and relax. The more you do this, the easier it becomes.*

Talk about the difference between watching and observing in Science lessons.

# Making glitter bottles

'It's so sparkly!'

**Make glitter bottles and use them to meditate.**

To make a glitter bottle, all you need to do is pour water into a plastic bottle but not right to the top, just most of the way up. Then tip in some glitter. Add a few drops of your favourite colour food colouring, then screw the lid on the bottle as tightly as you can. Use tape to seal the lid onto the bottle, making it waterproof.

Sit with a straight back and take a deep breath. Give your glitter bottle a shake. As the glitter whirls around, notice how much harder it is to see through the bottle. Let the glitter settle then give the bottle another big shake.

This time put your hand on your belly. Breathe slowly and deeply, feeling your breath on your hand. As the glitter settles keep feeling your slow breathing. Once the glitter has completely settled, everything is calm. You can see through the bottle clearly now.

Your thoughts are a bit like the glitter. When they race around, shaken up by the events in our lives, it's hard to see clearly. When we let our thoughts settle, and breathe slowly and calmly, we can see things much better. Take your glitter bottle home with you. Anytime you need to be calm and relaxed, repeat this exercise. Hold your belly and feel your breathing become slow and calm.

Make glitter bottles with your class and practise the breathing exercises. Adding a few drops of soap to a glitter bottle helps the glitter move around more slowly and evenly. You can also squeeze glitter glue into warm water. This gives a different movement in the water.

**Teaching tip**

To make the glitter bottles, you need small, empty plastic bottles, water, glitter, food colouring and tape to seal the lids. You could collect jars in the staffroom for this activity too as they have screw top lids which might mean fewer spillages.

# Fishing

'Gone fishin'.'

**Look at how going fishing is an art of relaxation.**

Lots of people who go fishing don't keep what they catch. They put the fish back once they have caught them. People who go fishing aren't always trying to catch fish for food. Instead, they go fishing to unwind and relax.

People who go fishing usually go into nature to do so. They find quiet spots along riverbanks, sit in the shade of a tree by a lake or stand on a pier at the beach. By going into nature, we are escaping the hustle and bustle of busy places. We are escaping crowds of people and all the noise this brings. We are finding a quiet place to sit back and relax, surrounded by beautiful scenery.

Even though fishing just involves sitting around and relaxing, it is very good for your physical health. You are outside connecting with nature, something that has positive effects on your physical and mental health. Fishing helps with your concentration too. Plus, being near water also has a calming effect on our bodies as it helps to lower our heart rate.

When we go fishing, we might catch something or we might not. It doesn't matter. It's the relaxation that is important. You don't even have to take any equipment. You might not even try and catch a fish. You might just sit by the water and relax. Try fishing without actually doing any fishing at all.

Recommend fishing without fishing to your class. Ask them to think about where they could do it and who they could go with.

# Pass the cup

'There's no 'I' in 'TEAM'.'

**Look at the importance of teamwork and ask the children to take part in an activity that requires concentration and cooperation.**

*You are going to be doing a teamwork activity in small groups. Threes and fours work well for this activity. In your groups, stand or sit in a circle. This is going to be a quiet activity with no talking. You are going to pass around a fairly full cup of water. Pass the cup to each other in one direction. As you pass the cup look at the person you are passing the cup to, and not at the cup of water. The person receiving the cup should also look at you and not at the cup. That's the important part.*

*There is no winner here. It isn't about who can pass the cup the fastest. It's all about working together as a team. Pass the cup slowly and don't drop it. Look at your partner and not at the cup. Feel that they have got it before you let go. Continue for a few minutes.*

*Next, repeat the exercise but with your eyes closed. Sit in a circle facing your team. You will need to tap the person you are passing the cup to but don't speak. With your eyes closed, your other senses are needed. Can you hear the other person move? Can you feel them touch your arm or hand? How will you make sure the water doesn't spill?*

*Once a few minutes have passed, stop passing the cup and open your eyes. Which group managed to not spill any water and how did they do it?*

Once you've completed the activity, discuss the best way to pass the cup without spilling any water. Ask the children to share strategies.

### Teaching tip

If this activity is too hard at first, start by passing a ball around before moving on to cups of water!

### Taking it further

This activity is all about working as a team and improving concentration skills. It helps children focus their attention on what they are doing in the present moment. The more they do this activity, the more their concentration skills are improved, so do it a few times with your class.

# How heavy is the glass?

'I'm stressed out!'

**Help the children to view stress as something that they can put down and walk away from.**

Hold a glass of water in your hand while reading this reflection.

*This glass of water is not heavy. I can hold it in my hand for a whole assembly or even a whole lesson. I might be able to hold it until break time. I might even be able to hold on to the glass all morning. But the longer I hold on to it, the heavier it becomes. My arms would begin to ache. My fingers would start to feel numb. The weight of the glass doesn't change and no more water is added and yet, it becomes heavier and heavier.*

*That's the way it is if we carry our problems around with us all day long. Our problems become stress and they feel heavier and heavier unless we put them down. Stress can affect us physically, just like holding the glass of water affects our arm and our fingers if we hold it for too long. The best way to stop this from happening is to put it down. Put it all down instead of carrying it around all day.*

*But how do we do that? I can put the glass of water down on a table. But how do we stop carrying our worries and our stress around all day? By talking to someone. When we talk to someone, we let go of some, or all, our anxiety and worry. We are putting our stress down.*

*Decide who you want to talk to. Put down the glass of stress to stop it becoming too heavy.*

Ask children who they have in their lives to talk to in order to 'put down' some of their stress.

# Animal meditation

'The love for all living creatures is the most noble attribute of man.'
Charles Darwin (Naturalist)

**Practise a guided meditation technique in which children imagine an animal.**

*Choose an animal. It could be your pet or an animal from the zoo. It could be an animal that you have read about or seen on TV.*

*Once you have chosen your animal, sit comfortably with a straight back. Close your eyes. Take a deep breath and hold it before letting it out slowly. Your next breath should be a little deeper. Take it down to the belly, hold it, and then let it go slowly. Take a third deep breath and this time think about your chosen animal. Keep your eyes closed the whole time. Breathe out and keep thinking about that animal. When you breathe in again, think about the fur or feathers. Does it have skin or scales? Does it have spots or stripes? As you imagine this, breathe out.*

*Breathe in again and this time think about the head or top part of the animal. Does it have ears? What about its mouth and nose? What does it eat? Breathe out. Breathe in and think about its arms or legs. Does it have claws or fingers? Breathe out. Breathe in and think about what it does. Does it like to run, jump or play? Does it like to hide or hunt? Breathe out.*

*Sit, breathing silently. Really allow the image of the animal to be there solidly in your mind. Then, open your eyes. The more you do this reflection, the better you will be at concentrating and relaxing.*

Next time you do it with your class, you could ask them to imagine an object instead.

### Taking it further

This activity is fantastic for children to practise concentration and focus skills. The more frequently they practise, the easier it is for them to use their imagination to picture any object.

# From worrier to warrior

'I feel so worried.'

**Look at strategies that help us to defeat our worries.**

The definition of a 'warrior' is a brave and experienced fighter. Sometimes, we all have to be warriors and fight our worries and emotions, so that we control them instead of them controlling us.

When we feel angry, we have to control our anger. Allow yourself to calm down and let the anger slip away, so that you are the boss, not your emotions.

If you make mistakes, don't give in to feeling sad. Fight that sadness. Tell yourself that it's OK to make mistakes. Mistakes are our greatest teachers. Learn from them. Discipline yourself to do better next time.

It's OK to feel scared about things. Being brave is facing that fear and overcoming it. This will give you the confidence to overcome difficulties in life. Then the next time you are faced with something scary, you will know that you are capable of doing it and you won't be as scared.

This is the way of the warrior. Be brave. Fight your fears. Overcome difficulties. Work as a team. Be the you you're meant to be.

Anxiety affects lots of children. As a teacher, you have the potential to help all of the children in your class overcome their fears and worries, especially about school life. Their experiences in your classroom can be a protective bubble from what's happening outside of school. Having designated lessons that help children's mental health is essential.

# The one-minute meditation

'Om.'

**A very fast, very simple, yet very effective breathing technique that can work well to alleviate stress.**

Stress is when you feel worried about what is happening in your life and you can't stop thinking about it. When you're stressed, it makes you breathe faster. Count how many times you breathe in one minute to find out if you are stressed. Some people breathe 20 to 30 times in one minute. If you are breathing like that, chances are you are stressed.

But, don't worry! This breathing exercise can help with that. It calms you down and makes you take longer, deeper and slower breaths. To do it, you need a one-minute timer. You are going to take a long, deep breath in. When you breathe out, you are going to make a long humming sound: hmmmmmmmmm. Like that. If you want to, you can open your mouth and make an 'o' sound then close it and make the long humming sound like this: ommmmmmmmmm. The sound is not meant to be loud. Just loud enough so you can hear it and feel it on your lips.

When you have no more air left inside your lungs, stop and take in another long, deep breath and repeat. You can count your breaths if you want to. Are you ready? Begin by taking in a super long, deep breath. Hold it for a moment. Let it go with a humming sound. Keep on going. Count your breaths. Breathing like this can help you feel less stressed so do it as often as you like whenever you are worried.

Counting your breath can be very useful to calm children down after break times or exciting activities.

**Taking it further**

Stress is a part of life and this breathing exercise can help with that. When you feel anxious or stressed, count your breaths. Slow them down. Do this one-minute breathing activity and get the breath under control. Make this breathing technique a habit in your classroom and your life.

# The wooden bird

'Ready. Aim. Fire.'

**Look at the Hindu story from the 'Mahabharata' about concentration.**

**Taking it further**

'Times Tables Rock Stars', 'Spelling Shed' and 'Accelerated Reader' websites all have goals to motivate children to succeed. First, read them the stories from the *Mahabharata* and other sources to inspire them to want to achieve their targets before they actually try.

*There is a story from ancient India about three brothers who are being instructed in archery by their master. The brothers have hit targets both moving and still. They have smashed bottles, split fruit and fired from horseback. But their master decides to try something else. Something that seems impossible. He ties a wooden bird high up in a leafy tree above a lake. Then he gathers the three brothers together and asks them to shoot the bird's eye. However, they are only to look at the reflection in the water and not directly at the bird.*

*The first brother steps forward with his bow and arrow ready.*

*"What do you see?" asks the master.*

*"The tree and the leaves reflected in the lake," the first brother answers.*

*"You are not ready," the master says and sends the first brother away.*

*The second brother places an arrow upon his bow.*

*"What do you see?" asks the master.*

*"I see the branch and the wooden bird reflected in the water."*

*"You are not ready," the master says and sends the second brother away.*

*The third brother steps up. He looks down at the lake and stares intently.*

*"What do you see?" asks the master.*

"The bird's eye," the third brother replies.

"Do you see anything else?"

"No, only the eye."

"You are ready. Shoot!" cries the master.

The third brother shoots his arrow and hits the wooden bird's eye.

*The story teaches us to not let anything distract us from our goals. The third brother only saw the target that he had to hit. He let all other distractions disappear. When you have a goal, focus on it. Whatever you want to do, imagine it happening. See it happen and make it happen. You can do it!*

The *Mahabharata For Children* is an accessible text full of parables. You can read these out to children to help to teach them how to achieve their goals and more.

# Use words sparingly

'You control your words.'

**Look at the power of remaining silent and the consequences of things we have said in anger.**

*You can't unsay things that you have said to people. Sometimes saying nothing is best.*

If this final idea is the only idea from this book of reflections that you remember, you have still taken one step closer to being the best you that you can be.

**Taking it further**

Read the recommended books and listen to the recommended podcasts at the end of the book to continue your journey of self-reflection.

**Bonus idea** ★

Review the themes and ideas in this book. Ask the children which strategies they still use. Suggest some other strategies that they could employ.

# Staying self-aware

There is, of course, repetition in this book. Repetition is the mother of learning. I wanted to deliver some key messages but present them in a variety of ways so that children could retain and apply them to their lives. These messages can change children's lives for the better, filling them with peace, hope, kindness, happiness, forgiveness, mercy and gentleness. Once they accept and live with those seven key components, they will find true bliss. As will you.

I hope that you and the children you work with have found the reflections useful and enjoyable. I also hope that you will continue to use the book with more children, spreading positivity and gratitude everywhere you go. Just remember to be here now and enjoy each opportunity the present moment offers you.

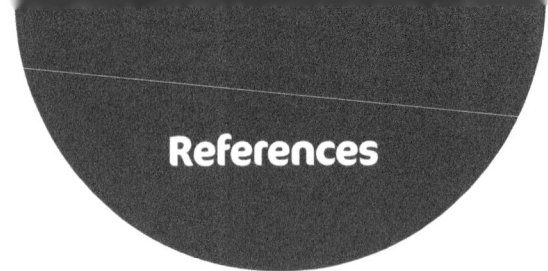

# References

## Books

Aurelius, M (2006) *Meditations* Penguin Classics: London

Epictetus (2008) *Discourses and Other Writings* Penguin Classics: London

Frank, A (2012) *The Diary of A Young Girl* Penguin: London

Holiday, R (2022) *Lives of the Stoics: The Art of Living from Zeno to Marcus Aurelius* Profile Books: London

Needleman, J (2008) *The Essential Marcus Aurelius* Penguin Putman: London

## Online articles

'Good Mental Health', *Action For Children*. www.actionforchildren.org.uk/our-work-and-impact/children-and-families/good-mental-health/ [accessed 26.2.23]

'How To Talk To Your Kids About Fake News', *BBC*. www.bbc.co.uk/bitesize/articles/zmvdd6f [accessed 21.9.22]

'10 Kids Memory Games To Help Improve Memory, Concentration and Thinking Skills', *Childhood 101*. www.childhood101.com/short-term-memory-games/ [accessed 26.3.23]

'Should I Let My Kid Climb Trees?', *The Conversation*. www.theconversation.com/should-i-let-my-kid-climb-trees-we-asked-five-experts-125871 [accessed 26.3.23]

'Want To Innovate? Science Says Daydream', *The Creativity Post*. www.creativitypost.com/article/want_to_innovate_science_says_daydream [accessed 26.3.23]

'About Stephen... And Fresh Starts', *Education World*. www.educationworld.com/a_curr/voice/voice129.shtml [accessed 12.1.22]

'Confucius Facts For Kids', *Kiddle*. https://kids.kiddle.co/Confucius [accessed 26.3.23]

'Forgiveness Facts For Kids', *Kiddle*. https://kids.kiddle.co/Forgiveness [accessed 12.1.22]

'Online Safety', *Kids Health*. www.kidshealth.org/en/kids/online-id.html [accessed 12.1.22]

'Protect your child', *Internet Matters*. www.internetmatters.org/issues/fake-news-and-misinformation-advice-hub/protecting-children-from-fake-news/ [accessed 29.5.23]

'Teaching Kids To Be Smart About Social Media', *Kids Health*. www.kidshealth.org/en/parents/social-media-smarts.html [accessed 12.1.22]

'Sleep', *Mentally Healthy Schools*. www.mentallyhealthyschools.org.uk/risks-and-protective-factors/lifestyle-factors/sleep/ [accessed 12.1.22]

'Slavery Resources', *Twinkl*. https://www.twinkl.co.uk/search?q=slavery [accessed 26.3.23]

'What Are Reasoning Skills?', *Twinkl*. www.twinkl.co.uk/teaching-wiki/reasoning-skills [accessed 1.12.22]

'Fake News', *Twinkl*. www.twinkl.co.uk/teaching-wiki/fake-news [accessed 21.9.22]

'Advice For Families Of People Who Use Drugs', *NHS*. www.nhs.uk/live-well/addiction-support/advice-for-the-families-of-drug-users/ [accessed 12.1.22]

'Gratitude and Prosociality: A Behavioural Economics and Psychometric Perspective', *University of Nottingham*. https://eprints.nottingham.ac.uk/39203/1/Thesis_LKM_7Dec.pdf [accessed 24.2.23]

## Websites

Free Rice https://freerice.com/ [accessed 24.2.23]

The Black Curriculum www.theblackcurriculum.com [accessed 6.6.23]

# Further reading

There have been many book recommendations for children throughout this book. Here are some book and podcast recommendations for adults should you wish to continue on your path towards wisdom.

**Books**

*365 Tao* by Deng Ming-Dao

*The Power of Now* by Eckhart Tolle

*A New Earth: Awakening to Your Life's Potential* by Eckhart Tolle

*Be Here Now* by Ram Dass

*Be Love Now* by Ram Dass

*Breath* by James Nestor

*Meditations* by Marcus Aurelius

*Polishing the Mirror* by Ram Dass

*The Art of Peace* by Morihei Ueshiba

*The Daily Stoic* by Ryan Holiday

*The Wim Hof Method* by Wim Hof

**Podcasts**

'10% Happier with Dan Harris'

'Eckhart Tolle: Essential Teachings'

'Life Lessons From Sport and Beyond'

'Modern Wisdom'

'Ram Dass Here and Now'

'The Daily Stoic with Ryan Holiday'

'The High Performance Podcast'

'Under the Skin with Russell Brand'